open

## Dedication

*To Claire, for taking me into my heart and
encouraging me to stay there ... all life is here.
Thank you, hun!*

# eoin mccabe
# open

How learning to live from the
heart changed everything,
and can for you too.

*Disclaimer*
The information in this book has been obtained from reliable sources. However, it is intended as a guideline only and should never be used as a replacement for consultation with your regular physician. While every effort has been made to ensure its accuracy, no responsibility for loss, damage or injury occasioned to any person acting or refraining from action as a result of information contained herein can be accepted by the the author.

First published in 2013 by
Eoin McCabe

| Paperback | ISBN: 978-1-909483-00-2 |
| Ebook – mobi format | ISBN: 978-1-909483-01-9 |
| Ebook – ePub format | ISBN: 978-1-909483-02-6 |

Produced by Kazoo Publishing Services
222 Beech Park, Lucan, Co. Dublin
www.kazoopublishing.com
Kazoo Publishing Services is not the publisher of this work. All rights and responsibilities pertaining to this work remain with Eoin McCabe.

*Kazoo offers independent authors a full range of publishing services. For further details visit www.kazoopublishing.com*
Cover design by Andrew Brown

Printed and bound by CPI Group (UK) Ltd, Croydon, CR0 4YY

# Contents

# SECTION THREE

# Acknowledgements

*The names of individuals used in this book have been changed to protect their privacy.*

I wish to pay thanks to those who supported the creation of this book, including Mark Wynne who was instrumental in kick-starting this journey by imposing structure and routine to keep me focused. Thanks to a special group of people who took the time to read the initial drafts providing valuable feedback which helped to transform the work – Philip Byrne, Caroline Currid, Marian Byrne, Pauline McEvoy, Ruth Ní Bhraonain, Julie Shiels, Anne Tannam and Veronica Canning. The insights in this book are the result of many relationships and experiences in my life. My friendship and working relationship with Adrian Mitchell is one such example that provided much in terms of insight, understanding and awareness through our many discussions and shared passions for self-development, coaching and self-awareness.

There are so many other friends and acquaintances I wish to thank who expressed their support and encouragement in the writing of this book. Thanks to James Sweetman, Muireann Fitzmaurice, Liz Barron, Francis Valloor, Sinéad Christian and the 'Click, Click' ladies who offered advice on publishing and other related issues. My gratitude to Patricia O'Reilly for her expertise in editing and proofreading the work. Thanks to Vanessa O'Loughlin, author and agent, who was a fantastic support and is responsible for getting the book published.

Thanks to all who trained on my coaching programmes, attended my seminars and those more courageous individuals who came to me for coaching; you have all taught me so much.

To Claire, my partner, who supported me fully by giving me the time, space and encouragement to complete the book. Her patience and love are what allowed me to see this journey through and for that I am eternally grateful. Also, to Josh my son, who has taught me so much about the topic of this book just by being himself – he is open, always.

## Introduction

This book has one message – live life from your heart!
Anthony De Mello put it more elegantly when he said
'There is only one necessity in life … to Love.' To be
open to life, to say yes to life each day, can be a real
challenge. Learning to live life from the heart is a lifelong
process. Many people avoid it and stay in their heads
managing, controlling and repressing. This is what I did
for decades. It seemed easier and safer to keep the heart
closed and protect myself from being hurt. The truth
however was that this approach to life was attracting
the very things I was trying to avoid. When I got tired of
trying to control my world in order to feel safe, tired of
living in my head and thinking too much, worrying and
tending towards paranoia, I became desperate enough
to do something different.

I decided to open up. I stepped out of my head
and into my body and my heart. This was a painfully
slow process in the beginning with huge resistance to
overcome. But I had started something I could not pull
back from. I had left my old comfort zone and was in a
kind of no man's land. I was walking into the unknown,
facing my deepest fears. It seemed I was finally taking
the journey that is open to all of us and is the essence

of what this life is about. The longest journey in this life is the one from the head to the heart and this is my account of that journey.

A closed mind cannot learn and a closed heart cannot love. There is no joy or happiness in being closed to life. All healing and learning occurs only when we are open. Learning as we go through life is essential. Every trip or journey we take in life teaches us things. The journey from the head to the heart offers many lessons, which allow us to live with greater ease and flow. Learning these lessons is a personal experience but the lessons themselves are universal. Heart living is experienced through the practice of these lessons and, equally, the lessons are the result of living from the heart. Self-awareness is an essential part of this process. Without it we miss the lessons and lose the learning. Consequently we continue to live life in a repetitive loop of frustrating mistakes and familiar patterns of self-sabotage. As the saying goes, 'If you keep doing what you have always done, you will keep getting what you have always gotten.' Too many of us live in the past by constantly repeating it. To change this it is essential we make raising our self-awareness a central part of our life plan.

Without self-awareness it is difficult to be heart centred. With awareness you have the choice to open your heart, to connect with or meet another person in your heart. This allows you to be non-judgemental, compassionate, accepting and forgiving. Life offers you countless opportunities to learn and grow in awareness. Everyone grows in terms of chronological age but real growth requires your co-operation. Growing through life with awareness and understanding is powerful and enriching.

This is not to say that life is easy. It's not; life is full of challenges. What matters is how you deal with them. The deeper your awareness is the more effective you are at responding to these challenges. I have learned much from my life challenges. I would have preferred to learn these life lessons relaxing on the couch watching a good movie and drinking wine. But unfortunately I can't learn about myself and life by simply repeating familiar limiting thought and behaviour patterns.

Each of us is strongly patterned. Most of what we do each day is habitual and rarely given much attention. To consciously create change of any kind in our lives we need to spot and challenge specific patterns. Unravelling the patterns that kept me head bound for so long was part of this process. Spotting and unravelling our behavioural and thought patterns requires a high degree of self-awareness. If we approach it from the perspective of the head we will expend a lot of effort and energy with limited success. If we approach it from the heart we are more likely to succeed and far less effort is required.

When you are open to learning from a personal experience you move beyond the usual politics and drama that people take as fact. You don't get side-tracked by the drama or story and are able to let the incident go by accepting the lesson inherent in it. This is bringing your heart into everyday life. It allows you to be more relaxed, joyful, playful and peaceful. Once in your heart you experience a connection with life that transcends all your doubts, fears and insecurities. You flow with life and your connections with others are enriching. Everyone has this choice.

Through sharing my own story and the lessons I have learned, as well as insights gained working with hundreds of people over the past twenty years as a coach, counsellor, trainer and teacher, I will show you how to learn from your experiences, how to gain the insights available to you in everyday life, how to look beyond the story or drama and work with life by living from the heart. Follow me on this path from the head to the heart creating an authentic relationship with life, one that is rewarding, fulfilling and intimate. Open up and allow life to flow through you.

The book is structured in three parts. Section one details the highlights of my life story. The content and drama of my life story are secondary to the deeper messages underneath. Defining moments and significant events are detailed to provide a context for the next two sections. Section two goes beyond the drama of my story, deconstructing it to identify the patterns of behaviours and thinking riddled throughout my life story. Here the process of discovering your patterns and the personal life lessons associated with them are described. Opportunities to stop and reflect are provided in this section to assist you in engaging with the process, making it more practical and meaningful in your own life. In section three a summary of the key life lessons from my own work and life experience are presented. These lessons are also strategies for living life from the heart. Exercises in the appendix build on the work initiated in the stop-and-reflect pieces of section two.

## Lessons from a slaughterhouse

As a six-year-old I spent many Saturday mornings standing in the doorway of my father's single-room slaughterhouse watching the cattle, pigs and sheep being killed and cut up for sale in our butcher shop at the other end of the yard. I was mesmerised by the sight of the animals being hauled up by their hind legs on chains, their bodies dangling from the ceiling, and the workmen slicing the bodies open from the groin to the neck with one long thrust. A cloud of steam would burst out of the gutted body with a gush of heat. The floor turned a crimson red, as the warm blood flowed, slowly clotting and brightening as the air mixed with it.

It was a fascinating show. The slaughterhouse reeked of fear. The animals waiting outside became agitated and unpredictable, smelling death around them. Their eyes wide with terror, their intense snorting, squealing and helpless howls as they were pushed into the killing space made me feel sorry for them. I hated seeing them so distressed. It was in this arena of death, where my family butchered farm animals for a living that I learned about the power and impact of fear.

That potent presence of fear, as witnessed in the slaughterhouse, stayed with me as I grew through life. Along with this was the sense that life was brutal and scary. Only when I consciously acknowledged this was I able to interpret them in a way that was no longer limiting.

The lesson I took from the slaughterhouse as a six-year-old was not what I chose to keep as a thirty-six-year-old. With awareness and understanding I was able to re-interpret the experiences and learn from them. Today the slaughterhouse taught me that life can be tough and merciless. I realised how easily I could identify with another's pain and fear. I learned that fear is always present within me and can cause me to lose control and stress out if I succumb to it. I learned that death, while inevitable, is not something to be afraid of or to ignore. I could use the fact that I will die as a source of motivation for creating the life I desire.

By choosing to look for the personal learning in my daily living I have stepped back from the reactive, fearful part of myself. Taking the learning from life each day rather than taking things personally has greatly increased my self-awareness and self-confidence. I can now accept the simple fact that in life shit happens, and it happens to everyone. What makes it unbearable is when I resist it or deny it. Once I accept what has happened, I ask myself, "What do I need to learn here to be able to let it go and move on?" then I do whatever feels right to move on.

Most of all, learning lessons from life has enabled me to accept myself, flaws and all. For too many years I focused on my weaknesses, my mistakes and faults. Consequently I felt insecure and inferior to everyone. Feeling this way resulted in poor decision making and limiting myself in a variety of ways to avoid rejection. I became an accomplished people-pleaser and hypersensitive to others' opinions of me. I was the ultimate Mr Nice Guy.

Living like this was demanding and stressful. I developed dysfunctional coping mechanisms such as binge drinking, comfort eating and hoarding. Eventually I got to a point where these coping attempts were causing me more stress than support. It took an emotional breakdown, a marriage failure and a spiritual crisis for me to finally wake-up and stare life in the face for the first time since those days in the slaughterhouse.

Since waking-up to this reality called life I have learned things about me that my ego is not and never will be happy about. I can see positive and negative aspects of myself both in myself and others. Engaging in a process of self-acceptance has taught me to become more compassionate and open. It has enabled me to be more understanding of others and more relaxed in myself. I have also stopped years of incessant seeking.

The seeking was the result of being locked into a view of life which perpetuated a drive to find the holy grail of enlightenment and spiritual freedom. While I believed

I was looking for Me; my life purpose, my connection to life or God, a feeling of bliss and oneness, I was also hiding from Me. I played a game of cat and mouse with Me for over thirty years; searching in the world outside me, never once going inside, the only place such answers could be. The game of hide and seek ended the day I started to turn inside and be with me.

The lessons I have learned and how I have learned them are explored and distilled into a set of universal life lessons in the following sections. I begin with my story. While my story is just that, a story, and we all have our own, the lessons learned are familiar and easy to identify with. My experience shows that no matter how bad things get, if you can find the personal learning in a situation then you have begun to let go of the ego reaction to it. Letting ego run your life is a recipe for misery and frustration. Another way of describing living from the ego is living in the head all the time, where everything is judged, analysed, labelled and controlled. There is no room for compassion, love, trust, forgiveness, fun.

In other words the heart is not open. The life lessons throughout this book show you how to bring your heart fully into your life and to release yourself from the grip of the ego. This is real freedom, enabling you to be more present, authentic, and ultimately more content.

# **Section** ONE

A Story:
The Naked Truth
of an Ordinary Life

## *Looking in all the wrong places*

Much of my life has revolved around self-discovery.
The meaning of life and how the universe works
intrigued me. I grew up fascinated with fantasy and
science fiction movies. I collected comics and books
on subjects such as ghosts, telekinesis, telepathy,
spontaneous human combustion, UFOs and the Loch
Ness Monster. In my late teens I progressed to books on
psychology and anthropology. I wanted to know more
about humans, how we worked, why we behaved as we
did. *Your Erroneous Zones* by Dr Wayne W Dyer was
the first positive psychology book I read. I was sixteen
years old. The fact that I mistakenly bought the book
thinking it was about your erogenous zones is of course
a minor detail now. My initial disappointment was soon
forgotten. This book showed me a new way of thinking.
I discovered how important my thinking and attitude
was. I learned about the futility of guilt and worry. I
discovered that fear was common to everyone and I

could change it. What a revelation. The book helped to sow the seeds of my passion for personal development.

For the next twenty years I was a seeker, constantly looking for answers. What was the secret to happiness? How could I have all I desired? What was my life purpose? Such questions drove my relentless pursuit for the truth. I was chasing after enlightenment. I felt like the Indiana Jones of the personal development world. Many times I thought that a technique or teacher or guru would fix me. I placed great hope in different teachings and teachers, only to be disappointed each time. Towards the end of my thirties I was exhausted and spiritually empty.

As a seeker I was addicted to feel-good tools, mantras, books and workshops. I saw this as the only work that mattered. I placed the pursuit of enlightenment above all other things in life, including living life! I put many people on a pedestal in my mind believing they had something I lacked and they could help me get that 'thing'. I spent a fortune on self-help books and courses, online programmes and DVDs, looking for the solution to my problems.

Some of the experiences provided temporary reprieve from the daily mental torture. However, I consistently reverted to my habitual ways of thinking, feeling and behaving. The cynic in me was stronger than the part of me that desired change. It was all too much effort and I wanted to find an approach that was easier and quicker than the last one.

I attended a shaman and read up on shamanism,

I did the totem pole process and connected with my power animals, I trained in reiki, I attended many psychics (one of whom told me I was going to marry the girl outside the room who had accompanied me to the reading. As the girl was my first cousin I dismissed this psychic as a complete charlatan and decided to ease off on the paranormal for a while), I attended healers and spiritual workers, learned meditation techniques and yoga. I dabbled in aura-soma, psychic healing, biodynamic therapy, emotional journey work and sound therapy. I explored Buddhism, learned and practised energy clearing, trained in counselling and as a coach, trained in NLP and Psych-K, and attended endless workshops and seminars delivered by many of the experts in the personal development world.

I was looking for answers externally. I wanted someone to tell me what to do or even better to do it for me and just fix me. I resisted going within and doing what was required to resolve my issues. After twenty years of seeking all I had to show for it was a library full of books, CDs and DVDs and thousands of electronic files. I had mountains of information but no answers.

Knowing myself and what I stood for was always a difficulty for me. I tended to ignore my internal compass as a means of navigating my life. Deciding simple things like which movie to see or shirt to wear could trigger anxiety and a need for someone else to decide for me. Such indecisiveness reinforced my belief that I was not ready to be responsible for my career and personal life. Who did I think I was? I hadn't a clue!

I found talking about personal things easy. It was one way of enhancing my self-awareness. Sometimes I shared too much, due to not listening to my gut and reading the situation accurately. My boundaries were rarely set down clearly and observed. Being so open left me vulnerable to negativity, hidden agendas and manipulation. In my need for acceptance I based my decisions on external feedback. I valued others' advice and opinions over my own. Dismissing my own inner guidance left me with a constant nagging that I was underachieving. I was holding myself back, wanting success but sabotaging myself through negative self-talk and procrastination. I was driving with one foot on the accelerator and the other on the brakes.

This tug of war inside was frustrating and draining. I never felt satisfied. It was like having a giant hole inside that was impossible to fill. Trying to fill the emptiness consumed me. It robbed me of any hope of feeling content. My refuge was food and drink – filling the hole with comfort food and numbing the dissatisfaction with alcohol.

I would have done anything to rid myself of this empty feeling. Trying to fix it or fill it fuelled the seeker in me. This constant seeking made me restless, and my wife would often ask, 'When will you just stop and enjoy what you have?; When will you ever be happy?' I told myself she didn't understand and that the problem was really with her. The search for happiness was my top priority. Throughout it all I rarely left the head. The seeking was an intellectual experience. I understood what I learned but embodied and lived little of it. My heart stayed closed. That was my real problem and until I addressed it nothing would change for me.

I used to believe that my need for answers was the result of being separated from my birth mother. The moment I was born I was taken away. She never got to hold me. I started life abandoned. For the first six weeks of my life I was in an orphanage where it was unlikely that I forged any sort of an emotional bond or innate sense of security with another human. Fear of abandonment became a major filter through which I lived my life. As I grew up it kept pulling me down into its narrow, restricted cage.

I gained an understanding of the psychology of abandonment from a variety of sources, including the scientist Dr Mario Martinez (known for his work in explaining the mystery of stigmata from a scientific-spiritual perspective based on the investigations he conducted for the Vatican, the BBC, and National Geographic). His work, Biocognitive Psychology, explores how the mind wounds and heals the body. He describes three primal wounds that we suffer in this life: shame, betrayal and abandonment. Each wound has its own unique features and patterns associated with it. One wound tends to dominate in our lives.

The wound is where action and change in response are required. It is a signpost to a new way of being. The idea that our greatest fear is the source of our greatest gift is not a new one. By facing the things we fear in life we become stronger. Knowing what is holding me back and why may be important, but this information is useless if I do not act. The understanding must inform my action so that I cease repeating old patterns which keep me stuck. Caroline Myss in her book *Anatomy of the Spirit* talks about learning from our wounds but not identifying with them. To be a victim to my wound is to be controlled by it. When I see myself through the lens of the wound of abandonment, then all that I do and say is coloured and influenced by it. I fear being abandoned on many levels and attempt to manage myself to minimise the risk of being abandoned in the future. I keep my wound alive by identifying with it and manifesting it in daily life in spite of myself. I must realise that I am not my wound; it is something that happened and I have choices in how to resolve it.

Fear of abandonment meant I avoided commitment and was addicted to disappointment. Girlfriends, work colleagues, friends came into my life promising so much, but delivering so little in the end. Such experiences brought up the wound, together with feelings of anger, bitterness, and disappointment. I was abandoning myself by living so much in my head and not in my body. I rarely listened to my heart. I was not good enough in my eyes and so I abandoned me. This was the root of the problem: I was lost to me.

Looking outside, blaming other people and circumstances failed to heal the wound. Healing could only come from within. The wound held the solution to its own cure; the healing was in the wound. Martinez's work provided me with a language to make sense of my life intellectually at least. But I still needed to find a way to be free of my insecurities, and so my seeking continued.

My childhood was an uncomplicated experience. I was never abused or severely traumatised (excluding the abandonment at birth of course!). I had a happy childhood. At the same time I was insecure and desperate to feel good enough. Underneath the noise and drama of everyday life was a constant feeling of unease. This was my basic state and I hated it. I wanted to "fix" myself and until I did I spent much of my life avoiding Me.

Being externally focused for so long only made things worse. Once I realised that in my past were scattered both the causes and solutions to my problems, I had some hope. With hindsight comes insight. I knew that if I failed to reflect on my life I would not discover the gems right there waiting to be found. I decided to do just that. I spent many months trawling through diaries and note pads that spanned some thirty years and began to see what was there all along. Patterns, blocks, opportunities and glaring blind spots jumped off the pages. I was finding Eoin and this was just the beginning.

### The shop-lifting, comfort-eating, fire starter

I discovered by accident I was adopted when I was six

years of age. Playing on the street where I lived with a bunch of kids one afternoon, one of them blurted it out. Being adopted himself, he had been told by his parents that I too was adopted. This was probably his parents' way of reassuring him that it was normal and nothing to feel ashamed about. I quizzed my mother about it immediately. I asked her if it was true. She told me it was, but that it did not mean I was not loved or looked on as being her real son. She was honest about it and answered my questions. Emotionally I did not know how to handle it and could not express the strong mix of emotions that filled up inside me.

I subsequently experienced a recurring nightmare for some weeks. There were no people; demons or even words in this nightmare. It was simply a feeling of being trapped or stuck in a small tight space and surrounded by feelings of no escape, despair, terror, pain, hate, panic. It was as if these feelings were sticky and clinging to me. I kept trying to move away from them, to escape, but it was impossible. There was no escape, there was no way out. I was trapped in a world of misery and pain.

It was not until my early thirties that I remembered this nightmare again and for the first time could make sense of it. When I was describing it to a family member the image of a womb came immediately to mind. With insight it made prefect sense. The nightmare was a memory of my time in the womb. These strong feelings and emotions were being experienced by me in the womb of my mother. They were possibly my mother's emotions. She was nineteen years old, pregnant and unmarried, in 1968 Ireland. None of her family had known she was pregnant and as soon as her boyfriend found out, he left her. So she was abandoned, frightened and anxious.

In the womb I was at the mercy of the roller coaster of emotions she must have been going through for those nine months. I took her emotions and pain to be my own and carried it through life as my own baggage. None of it is or was ever mine, it took many years to realise and accept this. Since then I have been fascinated by research and work that shows how life in the womb is impacted by the world outside it. The foetus in the womb is intricately connected to and influenced by, not just the mother's body, but also the environment and world the mother lives in and her emotions.

Discovering I was adopted triggered memories from my time in the womb, and being so young I had no language to describe my emotions. My subconscious used the recurring nightmare as the mechanism through which to process this information and handle the emotional impact. Within six months the nightmares ended and I became infatuated with fire for a couple of years. Playing with fire was thrilling and, in hindsight, a way of releasing anger. Amongst the many items burned were almost all my toys, my sister's dolls, my bedroom curtains, rubbish piles, old car wrecks and used tyres. I frequently singed the hair on our cats and dogs, and burned a stretch of roadside hedgerow, which the fire service extinguished.

I remember the day I burned out our hay shed. It

was small, nestled in under a roof covering a number of adjoining sheds filled with animals and animal feed. That evening, I was sitting alone on a bale of hay in the shed setting little fires and then quickly putting them out. This was exciting and the smell of burning hay filled the space around me, deepening my desire for more. Suddenly, I lost control of one fire, it spread quickly to the other bales and in the blink of an eye it was a roaring fire threatening to engulf every shed in our yard.

I panicked and ran down to the house to my mother and told her what was happening. She ran out and somehow managed to extinguish the fire. I went up to my room and hid under the blankets to await Dad's return. I was sure I would be severely punished. However, apart from my mother's initial anger, there were no repercussions. The guilt and shame I felt about it was more than enough to deal with. My parents were not into strict discipline, especially Dad. He preferred to let Mam be the disciplinarian, a role she played with reluctant enthusiasm.

Eventually the fire phase ended but the anger inside found other means of expression. We always had pets about the house. I played with the cats and dogs often. I never killed a pet but I was sometimes cruel, playing games such as tying spoons to the tails of the kittens and watching them race about the garden trying to escape from them. It all came to an abrupt end while playing with the family cat. Whirling her around the kitchen by her front paws I accidentally dislocated her left leg.

With the cat yowling in agony and me crying with guilt, Mam threw both of us into the car and headed for the local vet. Luckily on the way to the vet the cat popped her leg back in and recovered fully.

Many years later while I was attending a hypnotherapist, the incident of the cat's dislocated leg came back up with very strong emotions of guilt, regret and sadness. I was shocked at the strength of these emotions and at how deeply they had impacted me. It was associated with a limiting belief I had in my subconscious. The belief was that it was not safe for me to love others as someone will always get hurt. Realising this I could easily see with hindsight how this belief played out in my adult life, holding me back from opening up to others on so many occasions.

Venting my anger through an obsession with fire, and later, cruelty to the pets, was triggered by the realisation of being adopted. It had awakened within me strong emotions that as a six-year-old I struggled with. I had no understanding of them and no way of communicating them with parents who were themselves wary of delving too deep into the emotional side of life.

My adoptive parents were, in their own way, very loving people. Growing up I was always closer to my mother. I felt secure in her presence. I could tell her anything. I hated upsetting her. When she was happy, I was happy. When I was eleven I was holding a ladder steady for my mother who was standing on it changing a light-bulb. Suddenly the ladder collapsed. I jumped back and watched my mother fall, her head skimming the side of the old iron bath. She was hurt and in my mind fatally. I ran screaming from the room for help and was too afraid to go back in with my dad. I went to my bedroom, knelt down and prayed that my mother would be OK. I cried for hours and was in shock for some time after the incident. Apart from severe bruising my mother was fine. The event still sticks in my mind as if it happened yesterday. Mentally and emotionally she was a strong woman and in my eyes was the rock of the family. She was, and still is, a very independent and strong-minded lady.

Growing up Mam was a positive force in my life and encouraged me to dream big. She was better at showing her feelings than Dad. She excelled at showing love to us through food. As a self-employed business owner she was always busy. Mam loved to dance, play golf and, like Dad, was a voracious reader. My love for books was nurtured and reinforced by both parents. When I arrived into their lives as a six-week-old baby they were already married ten years and had very full social lives. She was in her late thirties and Dad was fifty when they adopted me. Becoming parents was a massive life change for them and one they managed successfully. This fact was a source of comfort for me in moments when I felt overwhelmed in the early days of becoming a father as I turned forty.

Mam stood by me in almost every decision I made, the

only exception being when I wanted to quit university. She stood by me as I returned to full-time education in the first year of my marriage, and years later when I walked out of my marriage. She financially supported my wife and me in buying a house. Mam's strength was very apparent during the last few years of my father's life. She held us together as Dad wasted away from stomach cancer.

Such resilience and strength of character came with a price. I rarely saw my mother cry or express anger. She was a very contained individual. Neither of my parents was good at expressing their feelings. Hugging and other public displays of affection were rare between them. My father was also poor at showing me physical affection. I grew up uncomfortable with my emotions and unsure of how to express them.

Some time after my marriage ended I had a son through a new relationship. We called him Josh and he was the trigger for change in many ways. Displays of affection from Mam became the norm when Josh arrived. I saw a side of her that I had forgotten and even doubted if it had ever existed. Having a grandchild was important for her. This was something she had wanted all the years I was married. The presence of Josh in our lives helped neutralise the pain and guilt of my marriage breakup. His presence lights my mother up and makes her young at heart again. He does this for all of us.

My mother and I are obsessive about food and hate waste. Like her I could be secretive and slow to share information. She encouraged me to trust my gut, work hard and follow my heart. She also instilled in me a massive dose of catholic guilt when she caught me pleasuring myself under the dining room table. I was six at the time. She told me I would go blind and suffer other horrible fates. In spite of the risks I continued to do it but no longer under the dining room table or on the rug in front of the fireplace.

My adoptive father was an honest man. He had a big heart and showed his love for his family by providing for us materially. He wanted the best for us and encouraged us to do our best. He was highly regarded in the community and was a successful businessman. While he was a popular man, he was soft in ways and was taken advantage of by some in business.

As a role model he demonstrated the importance of respecting and helping others, supporting family and being honest. His funeral was one of the largest I was ever at. Several hundred people attended. It was then that I realised the impact this man had had on so many. He had achieved this by being honest, kind and supportive. He was unassuming and sincere. He was never loud or boastful, ostentatious or very ambitious. He valued making a living in an honourable way and, above all else, family. He taught me so much by simply being himself.

I regret that I never got to know him as an adult. Dad died as I was turning twenty and for several years prior to his death he was a sick man. We discovered how bad things were in the summer of 1988 and by the end of that year he was gone. The stomach cancer ravaged his body leaving an empty shell of a man. Watching him die in his final months was horrible.

I shared with Dad a need to please and avoid conflict. With poor emotional intelligence I too relied on intellect to compensate. We shared a love of books, film and music. I owe him my eclectic taste in music, from Bing Crosby and Mario Lanza to old Irish ballads. The only time I heard him sing was when he was merry, which was very rare. A social drinker, after his second or third whiskey he would belt out the words to the one song he appeared to know, the Irish ballad 'Boolavogue'. Dad loved sports and all things agriculture. I had no interest in either.

Indirectly, he taught me the importance of following my passions in life. When Dad was thirteen years old his father died. As the only son, he had to leave school and take over the family business. His career was decided for him and his ambitions of being a doctor were over. He remained interested in all things medical and regularly read my school biology texts. His desire for me to pursue agriculture as a career only served to push me more in the direction of my passion. Dad viewed work as a means of providing security. He believed a career in agriculture would provide a solid future for his only son. This difference between us underpinned much of our arguing, which unfortunately became the norm in the last years of his life.

I entered the world of work as one of God's helpers. At least that was how it was sold to me when I was eight years old. I was made an altar boy in our local Catholic church. The ritual around serving mass appealed to me, as did the uniform. This comprised of a large white surplice which was worn like a sweater over a knee-length, bright red alb. I felt special and useful. My favourite task was doing the paton. The paton was a flat metal plate with a handle on it used for catching pieces of Communion that might fall from the priest's hand or recipient's mouth. I followed the priest from person to person holding the paton underneath the chin of each person as they received their Communion. My least favourite task was ringing the bell. I was terrified of getting my timing wrong. Such performance anxiety became a strong feature of my life as I got older.

I enjoyed being a server at mass so much that I contemplated becoming a priest. This option stayed with me well into my early teens. It was the overwhelming lust for the female form that convinced me it would never work. Chastity had no appeal. What attracted me to the priesthood was the bookish, solitary life, preaching from a height and being untouched by the everyday hassles. I saw it as a means to focus on study, research and a life of intellectual contemplation, alone and independent, while at the same time having status and respect. I liked the idea of living alone, where real intimacy could be avoided and instead focus on helping others, reading and learning, studying and preaching. Best of all I could dress in black every day of the week.

My perception of a priest's life exposed my desire for a refuge from the "real" world, a place where I could avoid committing to another person. I remember a priest coming to our school to talk about the priesthood as a career. I was ten years old and impressed with the image he painted of a priest's life. I went home and announced to my mother that I was joining the priesthood. As any intelligent parent would do, Mam listened and then told me why this would not happen yet. At least not until I was out of primary school.

With my plans delayed I satisfied myself with the monthly duties of an altar boy, playing a bit role on the altar, watching the star of the show, the priest, do his thing with a captive and obedient audience. After a while, as Mam knew I would, I forgot about this ambition and slipped back into the daily challenges of pre-teenage life in small town Ireland. Father Eoin was not to be, in the ecclesiastical sense at least.

Growing up in Tullow was an unsophisticated affair. Tullow was a small, rural market town which came alive at the weekends when the farming community descended on it for their weekly shopping. Many of my friends lived on the same street. Their parents also ran small retail outlets. We hung around in gangs, swimming and fishing with jam jars on string in the river, and playing war games with bamboo sticks. I enjoyed being part of a gang, even though deep down I always felt I did not really belong.

What was most important to me was getting on with people. At an early age I became skilled at conflict avoidance. I have been in only two physical fights, both with the same person. This reluctance to fight made me an attractive proposition for bullies. When I was ten years of age I was bullied by two classmates who forced me to hand over sweets and money. This lasted a couple of weeks. I told my mother, who phoned the bullies' mothers. The next day they were full of apologies, insisting that the mental torment and intimidation were just a bit of fun. We became friends, which was my pattern. I was easy to get on with, very likeable and willing to please.

My need to avoid conflict also meant that I tried to minimise it in others around me. I was drawn to befriending those who were ostracised by the majority because they appeared different. I had an affinity for the social misfits in school. I did my best to get them accepted. I was probably doing this for myself. If they were accepted then I too would feel I belonged. While I was never rejected by the majority I neither felt integrated with them, nor was I comfortable hanging around with the few who were rejected by the rest. I was caught between both worlds in the classroom, which served to reinforce my sense of isolation and detachment.

One of my favourite ways to escape from daily life was watching television. It dominated my leisure time from an early age. I had my favourite programmes and my favourite food to eat while watching them. After school each evening I sat down to programmes such as *Sesame Street, The Muppet Show, Little House on the Prairie, CHIPS, Knight Rider, Magnum PI, Hawaii Five-0, Star Trek* ... the list was long! I was a television fanatic. I had crisps, chocolate and soda-drinks while watching TV.

It seemed I was born to comfort eat. Most of this food was easily stolen from our grocery shop, usually without anyone else's knowledge. I must have cost my parents a small fortune in lost profits over those years of shoplifting. Daily, I comfort ate, stealing chocolate bars, crisps, soft drinks and later on, cigarettes. I didn't smoke until I was nineteen. But in the years between eight and eleven, I stole hundreds of cigarettes. My friends and I would spend Saturday afternoons pretending to smoke, feeling cool and sophisticated.

Inevitably, I progressed to bigger things. I, and some friends, decided to start shoplifting from a local supermarket. This ended when one of the gang got caught. He was the youngest. He put up no resistance, even naming us in the process of confessing. Unaware of this development, I was walking through the supermarket one evening when suddenly the owner and his assistant jumped out from behind an aisle and interrogated me on the spot. I wanted to die in that moment. Horror and terror raced through me as my little life flashed before my eyes. I crumbled and admitted to everything. I was sick at the thought of my parents being told and spent the next few days avoiding them, too scared to tell them what had happened. I knew they would be told by the owner of the supermarket. He was particularly angry with me, being the son of a colleague, stealing from him.

As the fear ate into me over the ensuing days, I retreated further into myself, hardly communicating with anyone. I shut down, walking around with my head hanging, feeling nothing but regret and shame for what I had done and what my parents would think of me when they found out. When I was stressed or worried, I shut down to the outside world and obsessed about my fears. Eventually, my mother asked what was wrong. I had become so quiet that she feared I was on drugs. I broke down and told my parents what had happened and how horrible I felt and sorry I was. Of course they were disappointed in me, but I think also relieved that it was not something more serious.

My mother was angry at the supermarket owner for handling it as he did. This was probably hurt pride on her part – but far be it from me to argue with her! Needless to say the episode woke me up to my errant ways and I never shoplifted again, outside of the family business. I continued to steal money from my parents to buy toys and comics. This compulsion to steal from them was driven by an even stronger need to hoard. I felt the need to have a stash of sweets and chocolate in my bedroom, far more than I could eat.

The hoarding lasted into my adulthood, changing from chocolates to books and information. Regardless of the item being hoarded, the purpose was always the same: to feel safe and in control. Thankfully I grew out of the desire to steal money. The feelings of insecurity and low self-confidence were present all through my youth and well into my adult life. The behaviours such as hoarding, stealing to buy things, comfort eating and spending so much time alone were ways of dealing with these feelings. I was trying to drown out or cover up the uncomfortable feelings by distracting myself with these habits.

For a while I indulged in a sort of impromptu, amateur feng shui, moving my bedroom furniture around the room. This helped me to feel good for a couple of days at most, the sense of being in a "new" space. But like all the other behaviours and habits, this was a band-aid, a poor attempt at numbing the real feelings inside of sadness and self-rejection. They served as a distraction only but never solved the root issue of my unhappiness.

## Maths, girls and the beetroot effect

My parents ran grocery and butcher shops side by side in the main street of the town. My mother managed the grocery shop six days a week, an average of ten hours per day, and twelve hours on Fridays and Saturdays. The grocery shop was a long-narrow room flanked on both sides with shelving from floor to ceiling. At the back of the shop was a door into a storeroom. The check-out counter was to the front of the shop inside the doorway, and behind it were the cigarettes, sweets and chocolates.

The butcher shop was another long room, but

brighter and less cluttered. A large cold room was at the back of the shop. Fresh meat hung from hooks in the ceiling and on the walls. Sawdust covered the floor and the smell of raw flesh filled the air. As a young boy I spent less time in the butcher shop. I hated the smell of raw meat, the blood and messy body parts, the noise of the cutting blades and the choppers against the wooden bench. The shops were separated by only a few feet but they felt like two different worlds.

I was more comfortable among the tinned and boxed consumable goods, the chocolate bars and Lucky Bags. I hated getting my hands dirty; even bagging the potatoes brought up resistance within me. But it was still better than bagging eyeballs and livers for customers' pets. The only work I remember doing in the butcher shop was making burgers and stacking the cold room with cuts of meat and animal body parts.

I was a shy young boy. Dealing with the public six days a week in our shops, it seemed as if everyone knew our business. As I got older and worked more often in the grocery shop I got used to dealing with the public and even learned to enjoy it. Some customers had a lasting impact on me such as old Mrs Shields, who always seemed to be in her late eighties. Almost daily she came in for her few items and would stand at the end of the counter chatting to me about nothing, commenting on all who passed by the shop window outside.

Mrs Shields was a chain smoker. From the corner of her mouth hung a cigarette, the ash getting longer, as she chatted and grinned at her own quips for what seemed like hours. I was mesmerized by the stick of ash hanging precariously from her mouth, amazed that it could last so long before falling to the ground. She never seemed to notice, or maybe didn't care, when it did come splattering down on the counter or floor, which I would have to clean up later.

Then there was Arthur Keegan, a full-time eccentric and part-time recluse. He lived alone two doors up past the grocery shop in what can only be described as a filthy, neglected hovel. He was a superb watchmaker and repairer. People from all over the country came to him with their clocks and watches for repair. Most mornings he slipped into the shop for a pint of milk and one or two eggs. He would fidget in an old sock from his pocket to extract the coins to pay for this food. Then he would leave, having said almost nothing, certainly nothing coherent. He dressed in the same clothes every day and never seemed comfortable being in others' company for more than a couple of minutes. He lived and died alone.

Every Christmas my parents brought him into our home on Christmas Day for dinner and drinks. He would spend the afternoon drinking whiskey and intermittently chatting to Dad, dressed in his long brown overcoat. He cut a sad and lonely figure, but one that fascinated me. Little did I know then, but I had a lot in common with him, much of which became apparent later as I began to make sense of my feelings and behaviours growing up.

Working in the shop taught me about people and, with

hindsight, about myself. When I was relaxed I enjoyed dealing with the customers, having a laugh and a chat. I connected with people and enjoyed helping them and laughing with them. At times I would forget this and focus on the annoying factors of the work such as the potato weighing, the late evenings and early mornings, the cranky and awkward customers and the small talk I would have to engage in with people I hardly knew.

I remember the banter and fun I had with those in the neighbouring shops. The lads in the butcher shop, the tailors next door, the owners of the shoe shop and jewellers across the street. On sunny days we all stood or sat outside our respective shops chatting and teasing each other. It was an informal gathering which would abruptly come to an end as soon as a customer stepped over one of our respective thresholds. This sense of community and familiarity with the other local businesses was enjoyable and helped me get through the working day.

The grocery shop lasted well into the 1990s and I worked in it at weekends and during holidays right up to the end. In the last few years of the business I resented my time there as it was by then a shadow of its former self in terms of the level of business activity. Its regular client base was dying out and the retail landscape was changing with more supermarkets and convenience stores opening. Reluctantly, my mother retired from the business in 1996. A self-employed businesswoman for most of her working life, it was a tough transition for her.

Dad sold the butcher shop in 1979, sparing me the "trauma" of spending my teenage years handling entrails and dealing in raw flesh. He turned his attention to farming. He owned farm land outside town. Like butchering, farming was not something close to my heart. I resented working on the family farm and this was a cause of much conflict with Dad.

Through hypnotherapy I discovered that I was angry at Dad for not being affectionate with me. As a young boy I was unaware of this need and unable to express it. In a separate process called journey work, I saw myself as a young boy being angry towards my parents for forcing me to wear wellington boots (for farm work). I wanted to be loved without having to wear the boots; I wanted their unconditional love. I burned the boots and asked to be loved just as I was.

My disdain for physical sports (and physical work) was matched only by my enthusiasm for television and eating my hoarded chocolate. I dreaded physical education class at school. Sports day, an annual event in my primary school, was hell. I felt incompetent, regardless of the sport. I had convinced myself that I was useless at team sports and did everything I could to avoid them.

When avoidance was not possible I "pretended" to play the game. This involved acting as if I wanted the ball to be thrown or kicked to me while running in the opposite direction of play. I tried to be invisible on the pitch, which was a reflection of how I behaved in my life. The worst place for me, where invisibility was not an option, was in goal. This was a traumatic position for me. My classmates soon realised that this was not a position for McCabe if they wanted to win (or even lose with dignity). So I opted out of sports at a very early age and threw myself into academic pursuits to compensate.

One academic subject I struggled with throughout my school life was mathematics. During part of my early years in primary school I developed a phobia of maths. I was terrified of being asked to solve a problem in front of the class and getting it wrong. My face would frequently turn red, which earned me the nickname Beetroot. As I became aware of my face heating up, the panic rose within me causing the redness to deepen to the point where I felt I might burst into flames. This fear of getting things wrong and being rejected stayed with me for much of my life. I can see and understand this now but as a ten-year-old boy in a class of twenty nine boys it was about being accepted. It got so bad that for a brief period I avoided school by faking illness.

My dislike of maths did not dampen my enthusiasm for making money. I can still see Dad's grin, and pride in his eyes, as I displayed my full money box after a successful day's business in my bedroom shop. The "shop" sold various items to the local kids. Dad was unaware of how I acquired some of this stock. Much of it consisted of my toys and comics, but I also sold my sister's toys and books. I doubt if Dad would have been as proud had he known that some of the stock was stolen and being sold to unsuspecting minors. My Dad could only see a budding entrepreneur.

I loved playing alone. I played with cardboard boxes from the grocery shop. I would get the biggest cardboard boxes available and create a house. I would cut out a door on one side and a number of windows on all four sides, which I could open and close from inside the box. This provided me with endless hours of fun. Once inside the box I felt comfortable, safe and relaxed. I fantasised about life "here" and projected my reality of what life was like outside to create a sense of security within. This idea would manifest itself in many other ways later in life, some destructive.

I even fantasised about having a telephone-box-like contraption in which I would drive around. This imaginary contraption was a cross between an old telephone kiosk and a city smart car. Fully mobile (it was on wheels and obviously motorised, not unlike Doctor Who's Tardis, a programme I never saw until I was in my twenties), I had the means to communicate with the world outside. This "box" had all the mod-cons of the time including a TV and an intercom system, food and water. It had a big window at the front with curtains on the inside for total privacy when necessary. In my box I had control and could avoid life as much as possible.

As I grew older I pulled back from life more. This retreat or disengagement was happening on many fronts and much of it was unconscious. I felt the need to protect myself, to communicate and behave towards others in ways that ensured I was not singled out. Any situation which held a risk of rejection as a result of failure, getting something wrong or simply just standing out from the crowd, I avoided as much as possible. It was safer to hide my true self from the world.

Growing up I enjoyed painting, drawing and was a talented piano player. I also learned to knit. I used to knit small scarves for my Action Man toys, having them wear bright red and green scarves with their military uniforms. This gave them the appearance of being well-adjusted, sensitive killers. These creative endeavours fell away one by one before the age of fourteen. I did not have the confidence to persist with any of them.

My attempts to pursue art as a subject in secondary school were scuppered by my mother. Convinced she was acting in my best interests, she requested that I be switched from art class to mechanical drawing. The drawing was seen as a male subject, more practical and, as my mother believed, would be relevant to my future career needs. I hated the subject from the moment I started and maintained this attitude for three years. I longed to be back in the art class where I was one of only two males in a class of almost thirty pupils.

Studying was easy and I was a conscientious student. I loved the sciences and classics, particularly Latin, history, geography and biology. I was not practical and failed woodwork exams. While I hated failing anything, I felt no remorse or shame about the woodwork as I reasoned it was a pointless and redundant subject for me.

As much as possible I continued to avoid sports in secondary school. There were other extra-curricular activities that I embraced. I joined the school choir and the school debating team. I enjoyed singing but debating became a passion. I tended towards bluntness in my style, which got a good reaction from the crowd. I debated in both Irish and English. This love of public speaking stayed with me throughout my subsequent career.

Some schooldays were memorable for all the wrong reasons; like the time my Latin teacher slapped me across the face, or when a friend and I broke a window in the school canteen while acting out scenes from the previous night's *Hawaii Five-0* episode on TV; or the day I was caught cheating in a science exam, or when I became a target of my English teacher's sarcastic and nasty comments (this lasted for the final two years of school). Overall though, my school life was normal and relatively stable. I managed to fit in, avoid conflict and achieve academically.

The teachers who most impressed me were my science teacher and history teacher. Both men seemed knowledgeable. They were down to earth and easy to get on with as long as you played within the rules. I admired them. However, they were in a minority. I had an Irish teacher who had a temper that would peel the paint off a lamp-post. He could let loose any moment. I prayed I would get the answers right to the questions he fired at the class like shards of glass. One maths teacher, who was non-communicative, gave feedback in the form of odd facial expressions and terse questions. My commerce teacher compensated for her lack of height with frequent bursts of rage. All in all a typical school with the usual mixed bag of teaching personalities.

My interest in the opposite sex developed as I approached my teens. My vivid imagination moved from boxes and mechanised telephone kiosks to girls in skirts and tight jumpers. As soon as I could I began to date. My first attempt was with a girl called Nora. I was eleven years old. I got a friend to go up to the front door of her house and ask for Nora. He was told to beat it by her father who later went to my father to complain about my unwelcome romantic advances. I was mad about Nora for several weeks. When I began secondary school I decided Ella was the one for me. In typical male pre-adolescent fashion I showed my strong attraction for her by tormenting her daily. I teased her and zealously stalked her for about six months before I finally got the hint. She was not interested in me.

Rejection also awaited me that summer on one of the Aran Islands in the Gaeltacht summer school. While there I became infatuated with a girl from Dublin. I decided I would ask her to go out with me. My strategy, which I used many times subsequently even though it never worked for me, was to get my cousin who was also in the summer camp to ask this girl if she would like to be my girlfriend. I can still see my cousin coming back with the answer and telling me a little too enthusiastically that she said no. Faking disinterest, I quietly had a meltdown inside. Then my cousin asked if I wanted to know the reason why. In that moment I did not care – the girl was not interested in me, I had been rejected and via my cousin at that, so how much worse could it get? My cousin told me anyway. The girl was not interested in me because she did not like my body.

I was a naïve, innocent, soft and highly insecure twelve-year-old boy. I was not even aware I had a body. And in that moment I was tossed into a whole new world. Suddenly, I knew that not only did I have a body but it was a crap body, and bodies really mattered to girls. I was beyond devastated and must have easily put on a stone in weight from all the chocolate bars I mind-numbingly consumed for the rest of my time in that beautiful rustic island summer camp. That episode sealed my relationship with and attitude towards my body. I accepted that girl's verdict on my body completely and spent the next twenty years trying to control it, ignore it, deny it, change it and avoid it.

Laura was my first real girlfriend. What I mean by "real" is that we actually went out together for some time. The preliminary harassing and teasing had worked its charms on Laura who eventually caved in and we dated for about three months. We were both twelve years old. She was a petite, long-brown-haired girl, quiet, very attractive and gentle. When the relationship ended I moved on to the next girl in my class. Her name was Sarah. She was good looking, tall, slim, confident and bubbly. I spent the next two years chasing Sarah and when I finally got into a relationship with her I had lost interest. Infatuation and youthful lust had dried up. We parted company weeks after getting together. After this I was like a headless chicken, running after anything that moved but lacking the confidence to act and ask girls out for fear of rejection.

Soon after Sarah and I broke up, Laura and I got back together. We stayed together until the end of secondary school, two years later. We were schoolyard sweethearts. I was besotted with her and couldn't be with her often enough during these latter school years. We spent lunch times and break times together. Most weekends we spent together going to the movies, cycling out country roads to be alone and hanging out around town together. We got used to being together. I threw myself headlong into the relationship. Everything I did revolved around it. This proved to be a pattern for me in relationships, becoming totally consumed and lost in them, clingy and emotionally needy.

I spent less and less time with my friends in school, to the extent that by the end of secondary school I had disconnected from all but one of the guys. There was nothing healthy about becoming so consumed in a relationship, losing myself in it. At that age I didn't know any better. I was happy to have a girlfriend, particularly one as attractive and intelligent as Laura. I loved being with her. I felt wanted and good enough. I could hold my head up high believing I was as good as the rest of the lads I called friends when I was with Laura.

My sense of self-worth and self-esteem came from being in this relationship. It was like a possession rather than an actual fluid, emotional connection. Something to manage, control and get pleasure from. On Friday nights we went to the local disco which was across the street from where I lived. During these nights Laura and I would sneak out of the disco to spend an hour together in the privacy of the back seat of Dad's car. Dad had agreed to park the car at the top of our lane close to the road to allow easy and quick access to it from the disco. He was amused by this semi-covert act of ours and I think probably very willing to provide the car for us as it meant that his son was not gay.

For a while he did have concerns that I may have been gay as I spent so much time hanging around with one guy in particular, who remains a close friend to this day. Several times Dad had walked into my bedroom and caught us in some compromising position wrestling each other, playing out some scene from *Star Wars*. So when Laura arrived on the scene Dad welcomed her with open arms. He had always encouraged me to throw myself into relationships with many women as I grew up, advising me to 'love 'em and leave 'em' with a mischievous look in his eyes.

Those Friday nights, in the back of Dad's car with Laura, were the highlight of my week. I became fixated on them and enthusiastic for as much action as possible in the car. The first time I touched her bare skin was in the back of the car and it felt like velvet, so warm and soft, it was a moment of pure heaven. After that I couldn't get enough of her and I was like a dog in heat around her most of the time. All I wanted was to feel her and kiss her. Her smell and her taste consumed my mind and always left me wanting more.

Laura eventually ended the relationship because she became fed up of me being too focused on the physical side of things. I was gutted. My way of coping with the breakup was to throw myself into books and study. At that time I was about to attend university, so I at least had something to distract me from the emotional fallout of the relationship ending.

While my second-level school days seemed full of nothing but Laura, everyday school stuff still had to be done. Towards the end I had to focus on choosing a career direction. This meant university for me and engaging with the college applications process. I spent a number of sessions with my career guidance counsellor trying to reconcile a conflict around the choices open to me. My first preference was psychology and failing this, an arts degree in history, english or philosophy. In spite of my fascination with the human mind and behaviour, I ended somewhere I had never anticipated. For the following five years I studied agricultural science, a course that I had absolutely no interest in.

The main reason I listed it as one of my college choices was to please my parents. Part of me always felt I was a disappointment to Dad. I struggled between wanting to please him and resisting working on the farm. Our competing agendas for me and my future created a block between us. It reminds me of Liam, a coaching client of mine who claimed he wanted to be the next Richard Branson. He desired massive financial success. Through the coaching he quickly realised that what he actually wanted was a real relationship with his father. The Richard Branson goal was merely his unconscious attempt to win his father's approval. I too valued my father's approval, so much so that I did the agricultural science degree.

My sessions with the school guidance counsellor were spent agonising over my college choices and my attempts to reconcile including agricultural science as one of those choices in spite of having no interest in it. I knew what I wanted to do but I did not have the confidence to go for it. For years afterwards I blamed my parents. True they wanted me to do agricultural science but I had a choice and I allowed myself to be swayed by their desires for me. They had my best interests at heart and felt that they knew what would be best as a career.

But ultimately I had made the choice and blaming my parents was simply a cop out. I had to stop playing the victim card. This experience of choosing and studying a course I had no interest in would have a major impact and influence on my later career in terms of the work I did and the approach I took. It taught me the importance of making career decisions primarily, if not exclusively, on what interests me. Do what you love to do. This was the message that was forcefully driven home through the farm work and summer jobs I did in my teenage years.

## Farming and other careers to avoid

Every weekend, throughout my teenage years, I was dragged out to the farm to herd the cattle, dose the sheep, feed the animals, bale hay and so on. On Saturday mornings Dad would wake me for this work. Such was my resistance that getting out of bed could take anything from fifteen minutes to over half an hour. It became a habit to react this way and at no time did I ever embrace the farm work with a sense of adventure or positive challenge or even just enjoy the satisfaction of physical work.

We almost always kept a pet sheepdog. One I fondly remember was Credo. I named him Credo (Latin for "I believe") as I wanted him to have a unique name unlike all the Sheps, Lassies and Blackies that had gone before him. He was a pedigree sheepdog and a great family pet. However, because we never had him properly trained as a sheepdog he failed to reach his potential. He liked to do his own thing when he got out on the farm. Often, when gathering the sheep into a pen, Credo would change strategy and suddenly start darting in and out through the carefully gathered group of sheep, dispersing them all over the field. No amount of screaming at the dog stopped him. He was in a world of his own, happily playing with the sheep. It would often take us an extra hour to undo the work the dog had done. I ended up running after the dog chasing the sheep, while Dad, in the car, sped across the field in an attempt to re-circle the sheep back in the direction of the pen.

Other times we would arrive on the farm with Credo on the back seat, mad with anticipation and excitement. The instant Dad opened the back door of the car to let him out, he would bolt down the field in the direction of the sheep, any sheep, oblivious to what we actually needed to do. As usual our screaming at him to stop and come back seemed only to spur him on. We would spend ages getting the dog back before we could focus on the task that had brought us out there in the first place.

The early jobs I had outside of the family businesses included working in a livestock mart and a grain mill. They were summer jobs. Working one summer in each was enough to know they were not potential career options, the main problem being the physical aspect of the work. The grain mill appealed slightly more as I did enjoy operating the machinery such as the forklift and bulldozer.

When I started university I spent a couple of summers working as a teller in a branch of a large retail bank in a nearby town. I was excited about this work and believed it could be a career option. I liked the dress code (suit and tie), I had my own desk, it was indoors, work was paper-based and there were no sheep (or mad, frustrated sheepdogs). It was perfect. I performed well enough to be offered the same job the following summer.

I was made a teller from the start, dealing with the public and large amounts of cash. While this was daunting at first, I loved interacting with the public and my experience from my days in the family grocery shop stood to me. The challenge was balancing the cash at the end of each working day. On a few occasions my cash receipts failed to balance. This was not good. I had to exhaust all possibilities to identify where the discrepancy was. I remember on one occasion spending a Saturday driving around the countryside visiting bank customers from the previous business day asking them if I had accidentally given them too much cash in their transaction. I was searching for a lump sum of around €700, which to this day remains at large. I was bothered by such occurrences because it made me look sloppy and I was paranoid that staff in the branch may have thought I was stealing this money.

While I enjoyed my time in the bank, it became clear that a career in banking was not for me. I disliked the constant drive for meeting sales targets. The politics within the branch made me very uncomfortable and my poor attention to detail stressed me out more. So, like farming and all things agricultural, the financial services industry as a whole was a write-off career-wise.

The construction industry was also added to this list. In the summer of 1990 I spent a few weeks working on a building site in London. What I remember most about this time was the day we left work early to hit the local pub and watch Ireland play Romania in the World Cup. Ireland won on penalties and the whole pub went ballistic. I spent that night with my building-site workmates downing pints of beer, singing Irish rebel songs and old laments I had no idea I knew. That night I was everyone's friend and London was a great place to be. The next morning it was back on the Underground to the City and the building site. It was back-breaking work. The highlight of the day was the massive fry-up for breakfast when we arrived on site each morning. It was uphill from there. Coming home each evening I was fit for bed. It reinforced my resolve to find a career which required more mental than physical effort.

The summer jobs I had while attending university served a common purpose. They reminded me of the importance of finding a career that I was genuinely interested in and never to compromise on the belief that working at what you love was a real option. The fact that I was studying for a degree that I had no interest in also served to strengthen my commitment to pursue only what my heart wanted as a career once I graduated.

In university I continued to operate within my comfort zone focusing almost exclusively on the academic side of college life. The first year was spent mainly in lectures, the college library and my bedroom studying. I socialised little, if I could go back in time now I would party more. I was too cautious and rigidly stuck to the routines I had created around studying and attending lectures.

The curious thing about this first year was how I chose to highlight, subconsciously, the fact that I felt like an outsider amongst my agriculture faculty peers. I wore a hat. Not a farmer's cap but the type worn in the 1940s detective movies, with Humphrey Bogart and Spencer Tracy. I looked like an extra who had just walked off the set of *The Untouchables*. Apart from the Students' Union President, I was the only one who wore such a hat on campus. In spite of the fact that I was very self-conscious about wearing it, something inside me felt compelled to do this.

The hat did not survive beyond first year. In spite of my attempt to distance myself from the other agricultural students, I made some friends, which helped me to stay in the degree programme initially. I tried to quit about half way through when my Dad died in 1988. I saw his death as an opportunity to get out, as the fear of disappointing him was now gone. However, I had not banked on my mother's incredible ability to emotionally hold me to account. So I finished my degree. I focused on one set of exams at a time, semester by semester, year by year and completed with honours. Having performed well in a course that I disliked gave me a great sense of achievement and showed me that I was capable of being focused and determined.

After first year I even began to have a social life, tame in comparison to my peers but progress for me. Part of the degree required students to spend a year learning the practical side of agricultural science – In other words working on an actual farm. Having spent most of my youth avoiding farm work I was not about to give in now. I opted instead to go to agricultural college for the year. Here men and women were trained in the technical skills of farming. Unlike university, this was vocational education catering for future farmers and farm workers regardless of their education levels. Facing into a year of practical farm work had every cell in my body cringing. The year was bearable because some of my university friends were with me. Being such a small group, eight university students in a larger group of about forty, we stood out in the college.

As a rule, students in the agricultural science faculty were known in the university for being dedicated party animals. This reputation was also true of the students in the agricultural college, although the drinking was more sporadic and intense. I remember joyriding in a tractor with two other classmates (the three of us squeezed into the cab) one Sunday afternoon on the college farm. We were nearly fried as the front loader narrowly missed an overhead power line by a few inches.

On another occasion I broke my left heel bone while jumping from the back of a moving trailer. The final five months of my time in the college were on crutches. While this did not hinder my enthusiasm for drinking and partying, it did lessen my ability to partake in the practical exercises in the school. On the final day of that year I handed the crutches back to the college principal and walked out of the place a free man, vowing never to set foot in a field or put my arm up the rear end of a cow again.

One of the activities that helped me to stay sane during that year in college was the decision a university friend and I made to take over the college shop with a bank loan. We became the proud owners of the college sweet (and cigarette) shop for the academic year. For me it was an escape from the student population and from general agricultural college life. We failed to make a profit by the end of the year, mainly because we ate too much of the stock.

The college shop was a welcome refuge for me after Dad died. He died on Christmas night. I came back to college a few weeks after the funeral and hibernated in my room and in the college shop. I felt lost and unsure of myself. Emotionally I went cold. I used his death to gain sympathy and to avoid partaking in practical classes in the afternoons.

The agricultural college took us on a European tour to Austria and Germany towards the end of the academic year. Many commented on how nimble and light I had become on the crutches. I was up on the ski slopes of Innsbruck and I explored Belsen concentration camp memorial. We drank ourselves into oblivion in Oberammergau and spent a fortune on porn magazines in Munich. By now the college staff knew what my fellow students had known for sometime: the crutches were being used as a convenient excuse to avoid participation in the practical classes.

That year was my worst so far. I hated being in college. I had broken my heel bone and worst of all I had lost my father. Also, I had used Dad's death and my injury to avoid as much college work as possible. I was absent the day the class photo was taken. This seemed appropriate, as I was certainly absent emotionally and sometimes physically for much of that year.

I returned to university the following autumn for two final years. It was a relief to be free of the farm work and the practical training sessions, and get back to reading books and learning theory. I did what I had to do to get through. I had to focus on my future career. Now that I was grown up, what would I do for the rest of my life? I had no clue. I knew what I did not want, which was anything related to agriculture.

In the end the only acceptable option was to go into education. I would become a second-level teacher. I went on to complete the post-graduate diploma in education. I had spent the past five years studying subjects in which I had no interest. Now I felt as if I had paid my debt or done my duty by completing the agricultural science degree, the world was mine to explore in whatever way I saw fit. I was determined that from now on I would choose what I was interested in and not be influenced by others.

So far my university experience had taught me the importance of taking full responsibility for my own career and life decisions. However, it seemed I had learned little about how relationships with the opposite sex worked. University had failed to deliver the sexual freedom and exploration I had hoped for. I graduated from UCD with plenty of knowledge in my head, but when it came to love and sex I was still that insecure young man blissfully unaware of how much I did not know.

While in university I had very few girlfriends. As before, the relationships I did have were very intense and all-consuming. I had the rare one night stand, but these were of little interest to me. I wanted a relationship. With a relationship I could create a space where I felt safe and secure. I wanted a relationship to help me feel good about myself. During this period I met a girl from the law faculty. Her name was Jane and she was a freshman. She actually approached me at a disco and all but told me she wanted to go out with me. Relieved that rejection was not a possibility and so flattered by her attention I jumped at the opportunity. She was a breath of fresh air. She was younger than me, very attractive, intelligent, lively, adventurous and vivacious.

I was both challenged and excited by Jane who seemed to have no inhibitions. She loved kissing in public, which initially used to freak me out, feeling so self conscious. As was my tendency in a relationship, I neglected my regular friendships with the lads and even skipped lectures to be with her. Once again I was losing me to be with her. We got on magically for the first few months and then at the end of the sixth month she broke it off, explaining that I was too controlling. I had no idea what she meant by this and thought the girl was nuts. The weekend of the break-up I cried right up until Monday! Then I felt I was over her. I was surprised how quickly I had recovered. I can now see what Jane meant by "too controlling". Wanting to be with her so much was smothering her. I was too clingy, too needy.

During my teens and twenties, I was very shy and lacked confidence in approaching girls for dates. On the rare occasion when I did build up the courage to ask out a girl I had the uncanny knack of picking one who was not attracted to me. This served as evidence that I was not good looking and that girls were not interested in me romantically. I felt that I was lucky to be in a relationship when it happened.

In nightclubs I often played a game of trying to catch the eye of a girl I liked to see if we connected on an eye-contact level. If we did, I got my thrill, I had "scored" and could move on to the next one. That was the extent of my courage and confidence. I rarely actually asked a girl out. Those nights out were often very stressful. Having such a negative attitude towards myself, feeling unattractive and terrified of rejection, I usually took refuge in drink.

Drinking and smoking developed in earnest for me when I was at university. They served as a limited form of comfort for the lack of female love interest. Looking back at those years it was easy to see the many potential opportunities for romantic encounters I missed or ignored. I was afraid of being rejected, so I decided the best thing to do was to do nothing, risk nothing. So I lived in the cinema and pubs with the lads. I believed that relationships were great if they happened to me, like with Jane, but unfortunately she was an exception to the rule.

## Stumbling into my passion – a career path less travelled

In 1991 I trained as a second-level teacher in Trinity College Dublin. This year was bliss compared to the previous five years studying agricultural science. The course subjects were interesting and I often found myself in bookshops buying texts related to the psychology and philosophy of education. Educational theory and educational psychology fascinated me. I became enthusiastic about teaching and for some time, saw it as my calling.

My teacher training was in a convent school in South Dublin. I realised that if I could survive this teaching environment I would be OK in most schools. My first class was a group of thirty thirteen-year-old girls. We were all new in the school. I went into the classroom trying to look authoritarian and tough. As I started talking to them I developed a strong twitch in my neck. This had never happened to me before and I began to panic.

Instinctively, I turned my head to the left facing toward the only window in the room. This seemed to bring the twitch under control. The rest of that class I spent "teaching" while looking out through and talking at the classroom window. Not a promising start to my teaching career. That school year was challenging and uncomfortable. It was very hard to discipline and control the girls. Some of them, possibly sensing my need to be liked and accepted, had an amazing ability to manipulate me. That year eradicated any intentions I had of pursuing a teaching life.

With my primary degree I could teach a number of subjects to junior and senior pupils. Mathematics (in spite of my fraught relationship with the subject) and science were my main teaching subjects. For each of the four years I spent teaching, I was in a different school. The most memorable, even glamorous one was an international school in Switzerland.

I spent a year (1992/93) teaching biology and science to teenagers of wealthy families from around the world. The post also included housemaster duties. This involved living in a dormitory unit with a group of male students as their supervisor and disciplinarian. Each pupil had their own bedroom. My room was beside Dan's, who was an American teacher, a couple of years younger than me, also a housemaster and soon to become a good friend.

In the section of the school I worked in, known as the American School, it seemed as if the pupils' educational needs were secondary to public image and financial gain. Teaching resources were limited and the classrooms seemed to have been last refurbished in the 1970s. We soon realised that the school was all about making money and every pupil was seen as a lucrative cash cow. Any transgression of school rules led to fines being imposed on the student. Dan and I took advantage of our geographic location by hopping on a train at every opportunity and exploring as much of Europe as possible. Travelling became our top priority. In my free time, when not travelling, I developed a routine consisting largely of drinking coffee, smoking, eating Swiss chocolate and reading a book a week.

The school was on the outskirts of a large town. The walk to and from the town was scenic and in winter, covered in snow, very beautiful. One of the landmarks I passed on this walk was a cinema specialising in adult movies. It was one of a number of such operations in the town. I spent the year debating about whether to go to one of these cinemas and experience an adult movie on the big screen. I never did, because I was paranoid that I would be seen entering or exiting the cinema by one of the pupils. Worse still, I could find myself in the cinema sitting next to or near some of the pupils. It was not worth the potential embarrassment. So I stuck to mainstream movies and drinking with fellow teachers.

The fact that I never went skiing while living for the year in Switzerland is evidence of how rigid my routine was. There were limits to what I would try and skiing was too physical for me. The whole idea of having to "try" it, putting on the skis, dressing in the appropriate gear, all seemed like too much effort. I did try cannabis though. I smoked it on two occasions, the first time it had no effect and on the second occasion I felt sick. I stayed with alcohol as my way of relaxing.

The students were easy to get along with. Many of them were unhappy and took any opportunity to get drunk or stoned, not unlike the teaching staff. One guy in particular, who happened to be in my dormitory, was troubled. He regularly wrecked his bedroom and for hours would scream what I assumed were abusive rants, as it was all in German. He was a bitter, angry boy, whose home life was non-existent. His mother was dead and his father, living with another woman, had dumped him in the school only taking him home for the summer holidays. Most other pupils had the option of going home or to some location off campus on many of the weekends. I tried to befriend him as I felt sorry for him but I had also to remember that I was his housemaster and needed to keep a clear boundary for both of us.

In spite of being offered a second year to teach in the Swiss school I opted to return home. I took up a teaching position in the South-east of Ireland, again teaching science and being a housemaster. Here a teaching colleague and I were "affectionately" known as Seek and Destroy. I was, not surprisingly, Seek.

Sick to death of housemaster work, it was now time to live life free from pubescent teens whose sole purpose in life seemed to be testing boundaries. I was always anxious in case pupils in my care caused trouble. I feared this would make me appear weak and incompetent in the eyes of my fellow teachers. The need to maintain control was a top priority for me and the associated pressure was significant. Dropping the role of housemaster helped. Things became less intense then.

In my fourth year of teaching I was in a single sex

(male) school again. This was a day school and so finally I had a life outside of school hours. Maintaining discipline was more of a challenge here. I coped with this by exerting even greater control in my private life. An example of this control was my lunch. Every school day I made the same sandwich for lunch. This was often the highlight of my working day. It was a refuge from the unpredictability of the classroom. Lunch was familiar, certain and reassuring. This need for control dominated my life. I socialised little during the week and failed to bond with many of the other teachers.

At the time I was unaware of how rigid my living had become. Such need for control showed how unhappy I was. I was in a job that required me to be assertive and dominant over pupils. While I did my best to maintain control, and mostly succeeded, I found the process stressful and dreaded Mondays bringing with them another week of unknown challenges and potential confrontations. This underlying fear of conflict was present throughout my time teaching. It impacted on my ability to commit to and enjoy the teaching. So much so that in spite of being asked to continue in my post for another year I opted in favour of returning to full-time education to train as a career guidance counsellor.

My over-controlling tendencies were an attempt at avoiding conflict. Unfortunately, this just resulted in more conflict appearing in my work. The people-pleaser in me hated disciplining pupils and this was a disaster as I allowed myself to be manipulated by certain pupils and even classes, in the hope of being accepted and liked as a teacher. I hoped if the pupils liked me then they would do as I asked and there would be no need to be authoritative.

I put huge pressure on myself to win over the pupils, to keep things moving smoothly and get the grades the system expected. Dealing with a disruptive pupil always brought up a mixture of anger, fear and panic within me. How some teachers dealt with this on a daily basis was beyond me. I decided that teaching was not a long-term career option for me. Life was too short to be this stressed. I was fed up letting my moods and state of mind be determined by what class I had next or how well or badly the last class had gone. My power was being given over entirely to the system and there was absolutely nothing healthy about that.

This period demonstrated how I lived my life from the outside in. My moods from day to day were at the mercy of events and experiences happening around me. In my misguided attempts to control my external environment, it was actually controlling me. I enjoyed working with the pupils and motivating them. What I wanted was to impact positively without enforcing discipline. Career guidance counselling offered this possibility. Working one-to-one with pupils, helping them build their self-confidence and choose careers that suited them felt right for me. Thus, I took the next step in my search for my ideal career.

Returning to full-time education in 1995 to study career guidance counselling was my best year in a university. I loved the course and was excited about the new career ahead of me. I had an appetite for information and books on the subjects, particularly vocational psychology, adolescent psychology and life-span development. I enjoyed learning about the various counselling theories and practising the counselling skills.

For the first time, I was beginning to connect with my passion. Things were coming full circle. I felt that I was rediscovering that part of me that had read the personal development and psychology books as a teenager in school. The part of me that knew what I wanted to pursue in my life, the part of me I had abandoned and ignored for so many years. I was finally connecting with him, albeit slowly.

When I graduated I had the choice of a number of career guidance jobs. I accepted a position within a school system in the midlands of Ireland. I was recently married and we wanted to live in the country. For the next five years I worked within the rural school system. I was the only guidance counsellor for five different schools. I had a great degree of autonomy in this work. Moving between schools allowed me greater flexibility in the nature and routine of my work than was the norm in the profession.

As a career guidance counsellor my work had two core elements, one was assisting pupils in making career related decisions for their future lives and the other was providing counselling support to pupils when needed. I threw myself into the work, spending long hours each evening preparing materials for students, compiling documents and research for school presentations, information evenings for students' parents. I was out of the classroom most of the time, working with pupils on a one-to-one basis. I regularly met with parents and dealt with the principals of each of the schools. In short I was running a service which I was responsible for, and with this came a sense of pride, duty and ownership which I had never experienced before.

When I was in the classroom I was concentrating on topics I was passionate about. I would spend these sessions talking to the pupils about their futures, their dreams and hopes, and realising their potential. These sessions were a mix of information-giving, challenging them to be courageous in their life choices and motivational in terms of how they viewed themselves and their futures. This was not always popular with the teaching staff. In some schools I got sarcastic comments about the notions I was putting in to the senior pupils' heads, letting them think they could do more than they were capable of. I found this attitude, so common and typical in the school system, to be disheartening and frustrating. I ignored it for much of the time, knowing that as a guidance counsellor who was only in each school for, at most, two days per week, I was not going to change it anytime soon. Nevertheless, my message to every pupil was to always base your career choice on what you are interested in. Whatever you do, do it because you love it. Having learned this lesson the hard way I felt I could legitimately teach others this.

Working between several schools meant I never fully

belonged to any one school or felt part of a particular staff. I made good friends in a couple of the schools over the five years but when I left the system there was no big leaving party, which was the norm for any teacher leaving a staff they had worked with for a number of years. Unsurprisingly, while I was disappointed by this, I was relieved that I would not have to endure being the centre of attention at such a party (an attitude which accounted for my preference to downplay my birthdays and avoid a stag night for my wedding).

During my time working as a guidance counsellor I achieved an old ambition. I entered into a Masters programme in Trinity College, which was a part-time three year postgraduate course. I enjoyed the experience of studying and researching material relevant to my work. I received my Master of Studies in education in 2000. It had been an academic goal; very much within my comfort zone. I continued to do other courses as part of my work in guidance counselling. One such course was in adult guidance management which led to a new career move.

In 2001 I left the school system to set up and manage a government-funded adult career guidance service. I was still working for the State education system, but my level of autonomy increased dramatically with this new venture. I was pioneering a county-wide career guidance service for adults. A similar service was already operating in some other counties on a pilot basis. As the project manager and career guidance counsellor, I, along with the information officer, developed the service over the following two years into a thriving and highly regarded adult guidance service.

The work focused on providing educational and career information, advice and guidance to adults throughout the county. I delivered workshops and information sessions to groups of employed, unemployed and retired adult learners and I also worked with prison inmates. The service was the first of its kind to deliver career guidance on site to prisoners. Once each week as part of my work I visited the inmates of both prisons in the county. I found these environments unsettling but the prisoners themselves were enjoyable to work with. I was fascinated by the political prisoners. I worked with many of them and often chatted with them about their lives and their futures.

I remember talking to one prisoner about his struggles with drugs and how he finally overcame them. When I asked him how he had succeeded when so many others in the prison had failed to quit, his reply was simple and obvious: 'They probably haven't suffered enough yet.' When I heard this it made perfect sense, and yet I would not have thought of it myself. I would have looked for more complicated, scientific reasons for staying addicted. It's about suffering and how much we are willing to endure before we say enough, and choose to change.

Running and managing the adult guidance service

gave me an appetite for self-employment. The service was very successful. This gave me a confidence boost and got me thinking about life outside the public sector. The work gave me the freedom to include personal development material in the workshops, talks and group work. I met some fascinating people during this time, each with their own incredible story. Most of these stories had a common thread running through them and that was a deep hunger to do what they loved in life.

Sam was a typical client of the service. He was twenty-three and had been looking forward to a promising career in sports. However, as a result of an accident in work in which his hand was severed at the wrist, all had changed. When he came to see me he had been in and out of hospital for surgery several times. His hand had been sown on with about 60 per cent mobility back. He was receiving intensive physiotherapy and had a gruelling exercise and rehabilitation programme to follow daily to rebuild the nerves and muscles of the hand. Since the accident he had stopped playing sports and was made redundant. Most of his time was spent at home thinking about how his life had changed so dramatically and, in his opinion, for the worse. He was depressed and saw little point in being hopeful or positive for the future.

As we talked about his ordeal I began to realise how intense and challenging the loss and subsequent reconnecting of the hand had truly been for Sam. For months he was in severe pain and tolerated long periods of deep frustration and slow progress, exercising each finger and each joint, willing them with his heart and mind to become strong and flexible again. He never gave up. His commitment and drive paid off. His hand was at a stage of regrowth and strength that amazed even his surgeon.

I pointed out to him that this level of focus, drive and determination showed that he could achieve anything to which he set his mind. He realised the experience had tested him like never before and that he had more than passed this test. In reflecting upon the past year and how he had overcome the challenge, Sam started to feel better about himself. Only then did he allow himself to begin considering his career options. His deep resolve and desire to achieve his career ambition became palpable as we focused on creating a career development plan for him. It was inspiring to work with someone who, in spite of his misfortune, was able to see beyond it and even embrace it as a means of self-motivation.

Bill was fifty-six and had just been made redundant from a semi-state company for which he had worked all his life. He had been a technical advisor and supervisor involved in training staff within the company for the previous five years. He loved working with people and was a very visual person. He was skilled in IT. In his career guidance session with me he was angry and quite negative about his future. He saw me as his last resort.

Despite being successful and good at his work he had few formal qualifications and a lot of his skills were developed on the job. He particularly enjoyed the training and induction of new staff. This was an area for which he himself had received no training and yet proved to be very successful at. He believed his job options were limited given his age and lack of formal qualifications. Highlighting and exploring all the skills he developed and utilised over the past thirty years Bill soon realised that he had a lot to offer any employer. With this realisation came the decision to focus on the skills he had enjoyed using the most, training and teaching others.

Bill decided to combine his favourite skills with his knowledge and interest in computers by doing a teacher training diploma in IT. Several months after this session, I met Bill again. He was busy teaching morning and night computer classes to adults and loved it. He felt alive and on purpose again, beginning a new career at fifty-six years of age. Not only that, during his IT training he had been diagnosed with cancer and underwent surgery to remove large masses of cancerous cells from his back. He told me that what helped him to stay strong, recover fully and find a new lease of life was his involvement in studying a course he was passionate about, which was leading him to a career that excited him.

Sam and Bill were typical examples of the range of people who used the guidance service. Each was inspirational in their own way. I worked with people from all backgrounds, all education levels and many nationalities. I had the privilege to meet and work with inspiring people such as Rotimi Adebari, who went on to become Ireland's first black town lord mayor. The adult guidance service was a personally rewarding experience. To those who knew me or knew of me through work I appeared to be on the road to success. However, something within me was still not content. I still felt restricted, not fully my own boss. This sense of limitation was highlighted by a training course I completed while still managing the guidance service. Taking this course was the beginning of massive change across my life.

Always looking to up-skill myself and add value to my work for clients in the guidance service, I had been exploring my options for further training. The obvious area was counselling. However, I had doubts that further training in counselling and psychotherapy was for me. One day a brochure arrived through my front door advertising a course I had never heard of. It was called Lifecoaching and was new to Ireland. I liked what I read and felt it was exactly what I had been looking for. It was a way of viewing life and one's potential in a more pro-active, positive and empowering way. It complimented what I was doing and would enable me to broaden my skills. I was anxious to work with the whole person and Lifecoaching offered this possibility. This short, non-academic programme, in contrast to all the other formal courses I had completed, had the greatest impact on my life.

It was a wake up call. I saw myself in ways I had never experienced before. The course helped me to identify much about my limiting patterns as well as various strategies with which to change or eradicate them. I felt invigorated and inspired by the content of the programme. This was something I did not want to leave behind at the end of the course. For me it was more than a course; this was a way of life. It was an attitude and an approach to living which promised to be far more peaceful and effortless than what I had experienced up to then. Doing this course was the beginning of a whole new chapter in my career and sowed the seeds for deeper change across all areas of my life over the next five years.

Upon completion of the coaching course I, along with three others from the course including the course tutor, set up a new coach training company. We wanted to create and deliver a professional coaching course superior to anything which existed in Ireland at that time. This was my first venture outside the public sector since I began my working life as a teacher ten years previously. It was an exciting time for us all. We had no idea if it would work and the only resources we had were the personal funds we each contributed.

In that first year we delivered one Lifecoach training course over eight weekends from October to May. We had thirty-two participants. The first time I stood up in front of this group to present was nerve-wracking. I felt like a fraud presenting to people on topics I was still learning about myself and on a programme which I had only recently completed. My shirt was drenched in sweat by the end of my presentation. Nevertheless, I was determined to keep going as it was something I felt was right for me. What helped me to face these challenges as a presenter on the coaching course was my decision to relax. I decided not to try and impress the trainees, but to simply be myself, to be real and honest in spite of my nerves. This slowly worked. I enjoyed the presenting more and more and felt alive every time I stood up in front of the group.

For two years I delivered coach training sessions twice a month, while also operating the adult guidance service during the week. They were intense and challenging years. Obviously a price had to be paid for such commitment, and it was inevitably my marriage that paid that price. In 2003, when our original coaching company folded, Adrian Mitchell and I set up the Irish Lifecoach Institute (ILI). It was at this point I had to decide whether to leave the career guidance service and public sector, and commit fully to our new coaching company or stay there and coach part-time at best. It was a decision I took with a mixed sense of fear and excitement. But when I listened to my gut I knew what had to be done. It felt right to move on.

So I remortgaged the house and left the guidance service in August 2003. I never regretted the decision. I initially went on a five-year leave of absence, which meant I could return to my public sector post at any time within the next five years. However, as I worked in the ILI and delivered our coaching course I realised that if I truly believed in what I was teaching, then why would I need the safety net of the five-years return option. I either believed I would make the ILI a success or I didn't. Seven months after leaving the public sector I handed in my resignation to the Department of Education. In March 2004 I became a free man, out in the big world of business and the private sector.

Adrian and I focused on creating a strong, high-quality coaching programme. We succeeded in this and garnered positive feedback on our coaching and coach training every year. The company became very successful and at one point had a contract training staff of thirteen, delivering our coaching programme nationwide. We became the largest coach training company in Ireland and highly regarded within the Irish coaching profession.

The work itself was, at its core, about personal development. Whether we were training groups on coaching courses aimed at the public, or running in-house training programmes in companies, the focus was always on the individual and their self-awareness. Given the nature and content of this work it was inevitable it would impact on me in terms of how I was living my life. A good coach should never shirk responsibility for his or her own personal, emotional and spiritual development. They view themselves as a constant work in progress. A coach, because of the nature of the work, must be a model for what they promote. Developing as a person and embracing personal growth challenges and opportunities were non-negotiable.

The work was intense and exhilarating. I loved it, particularly the coach training where I could present on topics I was passionate about, such as self-awareness, confidence building, positive thinking and emotional intelligence. The work allowed me to feed my incessant need to seek answers to life's greater challenges and mysteries. In other words, the search for enlightenment. Spirituality was the holy grail of the work for me. I could not get enough of it and the business coaching work held little interest for me. I would have gladly let go of all the business coaching and training and focused exclusively on the personal and spiritual development side of the work.

I found coaching to be a natural style of working for me. I enjoyed and was good at challenging a client, keeping them focused and facilitating them to clear the clutter from their mind so that they could view their situations clearly and effectively. Facilitating and training was both enjoyable and challenging. The course impacted hugely on those who completed it, many changing their careers, and even relationships during or soon after the course. This was not our main aim however; we wanted people to re-discover their potential for making positive change in their lives and to realise the power of living authentically.

Also the one-to-one coaching work was equally rewarding. It intrigued me that often the client's issues reflected what was or had been going on in my own life. One client, who I will name Amy, was six months unemployed when she came for coaching and had moved back home. She was fed up and taking her anger out on her parents. She had been adopted as a baby. When she was twenty-three she found her birth mother, but a few months later her birth mother died. Amy had not sought counselling or emotional support. Her strategy was to repress it all and get on with life. However, repression only delays the inevitable. It was no wonder she felt stuck in life. There was a strong resistance within her to grieve for the loss of her birth mother, both as an infant and later as an adult, all of which was keeping her stuck. It was a block to her progress, and until she allowed herself to grieve she could not move on.

Like Amy I had lived life denying my emotional pain around abandonment, adoption and loss. I was afraid of feeling the grief, of getting consumed and lost in it. Amy reminded me that I had yet to grieve. Her resistance to connecting with her feelings and pain mirrored my resistance to feeling my own. Such encounters in my coaching work encouraged me to be more pro-active with my own issues.

What intrigued me further about our work in the ILI was that the nature and manner in which we approached and applied coaching was identical to Eckhart Tolle's description of "being present" in his book *The Power of Now*. Once again I was reminded of my dream as a teenager of working in the area of self-development and positive psychology and now in my late thirties that ambition was being realised. This brought home to me how important it was to never give up, to never let go of my dreams. There was always a way to realise my deepest ambitions. With enough determination and patience anything was possible.

In December 2006 the idea of leaving the ILI hit me like a bolt out of the blue. The moment it came into my head, I felt excited. The following January, I told my ILI colleagues and they were stunned by the news. Adrian did not want me to leave and did his best to talk me out of the move. I thought I had made up my mind, that I was leaving and yet as the months progressed I seemed to be hesitating. The desire to leave and the fear of stepping into the unknown kept me paralysed. I agreed to take some time out during the summer of 2007 to get clarity on the issue and make a final decision when I returned in September.

However, soon after I returned to work in September 2007 events conspired against me leaving and I stayed with the company for another four years. During those years I went in and out of wanting to leave the ILI and fantasising about starting a new career as a personal development guru or spiritual teacher. People like Wayne Dyer, Marianne Williamson and Byron Katie reminded me of my longing to be a huge success, revered and admired by millions. I wanted to be Somebody, not just Me, I wanted to be more than Me, bigger than Me and have the world acknowledge that. Maybe then I would feel good enough.

When I finally left the ILI the inner longing for external recognition had subsided. I was aware of it and saw it for what it really was: me chasing after outer rewards of success and people's approval. The hunger for acceptance and love from others was pulling me away from my success and skills in the mistaken belief that something better lay ahead and away from what I was doing then. Until I could see and own my success and skills nothing would change for me. The last four years in the ILI were about this recognition.

Slowly I began to witness my own coaching skills, my ability to inspire others, my ability to challenge and energise groups in my seminars and trainings. All this I was acknowledging for the first time in my life. This was the difference that made all the difference, allowing me to follow my heart. I could now leave the ILI grateful for what it had given me and for how it had prepared me for the next phase of my career and life.

## Less head, more heart: making relationships work

It seemed my career was progressing and moving with some clear intention behind it. The same could not be said for my love life. After Jane broke up with me in university I flailed about for a few years trying desperately to get back into a relationship with someone. I got back in contact with Laura who was coming out of a relationship herself. Her relationship break-up was something I encouraged during our frequent phone chats. Soon after she broke up with her boyfriend I made my move. We were a couple again for the third time. This seemed like the right thing at the time, I wanted a relationship (nothing new there) and I still fancied her. Being back with Laura was comfortable and familiar – too familiar. My need to be in a relationship had partly, if not fully, driven me to go after one in a safe place, i.e. with Laura. We would continue through the next four years together, getting married in the summer of 1995.

Our wedding day was the hottest on record in Ireland. It was almost as if life was saying to me, 'You are now stepping from the frying pan into the fire.' The wedding was a resounding success from the point of view of having fun. The marriage less so. Marriage was not something I had looked for or even wanted. But being the person I was then, insecure and needy, it was no surprise that I went along with the conventional thinking that the next step in a relationship should be marriage. Nevertheless no one put a gun to my head to get engaged and married. If I had stopped to listen to myself during the year before the wedding I would have realised I was not ready for marriage. But I ignored this and went ahead regardless.

It was a tough lesson in my life. I married Laura because it was the easiest option to follow. It kept everyone happy and things continued on as before. The people pleaser in me was running the show and making the decisions. I had not the self-awareness or the confidence to follow my heart and end the relationship, or at the very least delay the wedding.

The marriage lasted almost eleven years. During this time I threw myself into my work. I became a workaholic and this stole quality time from the marriage. Laura and I grew apart, each focusing on our own careers. The fact that no children appeared exacerbated this trend. Even though we were comfortable in the safety of work, which allowed us to avoid opening up too much to each other, both of us knew there was something wrong in our relationship and neither of us was happy about it. At times Laura would complain about this situation and I would either get defensive or accept her argument and make promises about changing and making more of an effort to "love" her.

In truth I couldn't because I did not know how to. I did not love myself so how could I begin to love another? This both frustrated and angered me. I flipped between blaming Laura for our situation, thinking if only she would change then we could be happier, to blaming myself, feeling if I could just love her properly all would be well. What I now know is that I was doing the best I could at the time. I was terrified of commitment and of rejection. My career success provided me with a refuge, a safe place to hide and live in and I occupied that place willingly. I was unwilling to show real emotion to Laura. While I wanted us to be happy together, I was unable at the time to give her the love that both of us wanted. Many times during the marriage I found myself crying for no apparent reason, especially after a few glasses of wine. As the years went by I drank more and more, working up to two bottles of wine a night at the weekends. By then I knew things were bad and yet I still did nothing to change it. Towards the end we were in a sham of a marriage, both of us very unhappy and living separate lives.

In the summer of 2005 I went to Africa for a few weeks, working with a charity providing food, supplies and manual aid to poor rural communities in Mozambique. I travelled with a group of about fifteen people from Ireland and the UK. This was a change of environment, with no alcohol, no trashy food, no TV or any form of distraction. We worked with people in small rural communities, many of whom were dying from hunger and a range of diseases including AIDS.

One of the main activities we were involved in was building small shelters for locals to socialise in. The local people worked with us building the huts with mud and wood. It was intense physical labour. At first I wanted to avoid handling mud and making mud walls; the physicality of it was uncomfortable. But the alternative activity, which was playing games and organising activities for the local children, was even less appealing. So I reluctantly chose the mud work.

By the end of the first week I was building huts and playing with the children, and loving both. Africa had pulled me out of my head. I was going with the flow. I was surprised at how much fun I could have singing and laughing with others while throwing fists of mud onto wooden walls.

We carried out regular home visits, which involved bringing food, completing any domestic tasks and spending time with the ill. These visits were emotionally intense. I felt helpless and frustrated seeing their suffering. On a few occasions I was overwhelmed by the intensity of my emotions. I resisted feeling it fully for fear of breaking down and being seen as weak. In one village we could only play games with a few of the children as most were too weak from hunger to play.

In spite of having nothing materially, the Africans demonstrated such strength, a real sense of community and love which was inspirational. I often wanted to cry my heart out while there. It was my first encounter with a world where the human heart was strongly present in everyday life while surrounded by abject poverty, disease and death. They would sing with beaming smiles to welcome us as we arrived in their villages. They were totally present and real.

I found the African experience challenging, amazing and very revealing. Being with people, helping and supporting them, was wonderful. I saw clearly how I held back my emotions. The experience woke me up and opened my heart to some extent. I came home feeling alive and excited about life again. I was determined to make the marriage work.

Once back from Africa however, I quickly saw how distant Laura had become. She said her heart had shut down. She felt sad all the time and could feel no love for me, even though she knew she did love me. I felt helpless. Laura had disconnected from the marriage; things had gone full circle. My reluctance to open up and love her was now coming back at me. I was reaping the bitter fruits of what I had sown earlier in the marriage. I went into counselling and quickly saw how much I was repressing myself and avoiding feeling.

In therapy I began to connect with the feelings and emotions I had buried away for all or most of my life. There was now no doubt that I had never accepted myself. I gave my power away all the time, never saw the good I did and was blind to the positive perceptions others had of me. I rated myself as not important, not worthy, and without any power. In fact, some years earlier while doing an NLP course I remember having a negative reaction to the word "powerful". The exercise involved describing ourselves and examining our self-perception. Hearing the word "powerful" said aloud in relation to myself was an eye opener. I recoiled from the word as if it was some kind of infectious disease, I wanted nothing to do with it and saw it as alien to me. Not seeing myself as powerful or owning my power, it was no wonder I readily gave it away at every opportunity.

I rejected me and my ideas, before anyone else could. I wanted to be accepted by others as this was the only way I could feel any acceptance. To achieve this I used humour, misplaced humility and a multitude of people-pleasing approaches. The fear of letting go and really living was too strong. The inner conflict I felt seemed to be between my fear and my power. I was afraid of my power and so repressed it by judging it, denying it and staying disconnected from it, thereby feeling lost and empty, denying myself.

These therapy sessions proved pivotal to my awakening. I gained significant insight into my deepest thoughts and attitudes. I was shocked and horrified to discover the intensity of the self-loathing and the extent to which I lived in absolute dread and fear. I hated myself and I truly believed that I did not deserve to live. Deep down I felt that I was playing a waiting game, just putting in time; I didn't belong here; I should be dead, gone; I was taking up too much space; I was not worthy of life in any form. It was shocking and horrifying to realise that these were the basic beliefs from which I operated in life. In hindsight it was incredible I had never contemplated suicide, but maybe that was just another commitment I was unwilling to make.

One result from this period of therapy was a decision to fully commit to Me, to realise my potential in spite of the fear of losing control and rejection by others. I was stunned by how much of a stranger I was to myself. I had lived at a distance from myself all along, not allowing myself to engage and enjoy life fully. Given that I am the only person I will ever be with constantly, and will sleep with every night till I die, it surely makes sense for me to finally get to know and accept myself.

A couple of months after coming back from Africa, and after realising how bad things were in the marriage, as well as within myself through the therapy, I took some quiet time alone for a couple of days in Sligo to decide whether to stay in the marriage. I had my old diaries and journals to help me reflect and get some perspective. My regular journaling throughout my past proved to be a powerful way of revealing the truth to myself. Personal patterns and agendas became clear to me. Assuming you are being honest, there is no hiding place on paper. The journals helped to confirm what I suspected at a gut level for some time.

The marriage was the clearest mirror for my unhappiness. In the marriage there was never any real lasting intimacy or open affection between us. We both behaved in ways (mainly subconsciously) that maintained the status quo of distance, coldness and blame with only moments of connection and openness. In my journals I came across as very frustrated, tortured, angry and scared. Throughout my time in Sligo, I prayed, meditated and journalled, asked for guidance and clear signs of what to do. In the end the decision was easy and felt right. I had to end the marriage for both our sakes.

Returning home I told Laura my decision. The ensuing conversation was a very emotional one. But we had a real conversation for the first time in a long time. It was not clouded with hidden agendas, underlying frustrations, judgements or resentments. We were honest with each other. The outcome was we agreed to stay together until after Christmas at least and enter into marriage counselling. Such real conversations became more frequent between us over the following months as we engaged in the counselling process.

As our counselling sessions progressed it served to highlight even more the extent to which we had grown apart. Eventually I moved out in March 2006. The day

I left was the worst day of my life. I felt like I was being ripped open and decimated from the core of my being. I howled and roared tears of pain and loss driving away from Laura and the only life I knew. Without doubt leaving the marriage was one of the toughest challenges I have ever had to face. I was in shock for months afterwards and wracked with guilt. I often contemplated going back, terrified I had done the wrong thing.

In some ways the marriage had been a hiding place from life. I felt so unworthy of love and happiness that I had hidden away in a shadow of a marriage for many years, playing happy family and successful suburbanite. I certainly achieved a lot by society's standards, but I never felt I was doing well enough or was good enough. This was in spite of the feedback from family, friends and work colleagues who saw potential in me for doing greater things. I rarely saw this in myself and the odd time that I did, it was quickly discounted.

I was too focused on fear and self doubt. My fear of rejection kept me in the marriage. Not wanting to be abandoned meant that I would never abandon. My poor emotional commitment was what actually helped ensure the destruction of the marriage. I failed to commit emotionally. There was a lack of intimacy and no relationship can last without intimacy. At best we were close friends, but in the end this was not enough to keep us together. Once I could see what I was doing and how I was in the marriage, I knew it made no sense to stay and continue to live a lie. This charade had to end if I was to free myself from the bondage of these miserable limiting beliefs.

Hiding away in the marriage meant I didn't have to deal with my lack of self-confidence, my deep inner fears and self-loathing. I saw Laura as the one with issues, thinking if only she would get herself sorted then we would be OK and things would be better in the marriage. There was nothing wrong with me. After all I was self-aware and knew all about personal development, or so I thought. I believed this for many years. No relationship could survive such arrogance and ignorance.

As a way of coping with this stress I stopped feeling any so called negative feelings such as discomfort, fear, or sadness. I told myself I was above such feelings. I had decided that feelings such as frustration, anger, sadness or unhappiness were irrelevant to me because my work was focused on helping people to be positive and confident. Therefore I had to be positive and happy. This denial served to worsen things for me emotionally and to intensify the negative patterns of behaviour I was experiencing on a daily basis.

I eventually realised that I needed to let myself feel these feelings and not judge or avoid them. Not letting myself feel was a form of bullying or self-manipulation. Such behaviour was mirrored in my relationship with Laura. With hindsight it became clear that I was bullying Laura during the marriage. Not in any deliberate, overt way. It took the form of being distant, cold, condescending, judgemental, thinking I knew what was best for her by telling her to read certain books, to change her thinking or attitude, being pushy in an effort to make her more like how I thought she needed to be. Such contempt clearly showed how I perceived and treated myself also. I was demanding and hard on myself, feeling I never had enough time to do what I felt I wanted and needed to do, putting myself under excessive pressure and stressing out.

There was an underlying sense of frustration and anger within me which I often directed at Laura (but increasingly against myself towards the end of the marriage). These emotions and behaviours had a devastating impact on the physical aspect of the relationship. The lack of physical and emotional intimacy between us seemed to both fuel the feelings of frustration and anger, as well as being the consequence of them.

Walking out of the marriage felt like a powerful breaking of the fear-laden chains I had tied myself down with. I had ended the misery at thirty-six years of age and only then did my life really begin to blossom. All the personal development work I had done and learned was now coming home for practical application. The problem was me. I needed to start looking inwards rather than out at others and blaming them for my misery. No more theorising and intellectualising, no more hiding. It was the beginning of me committing to myself. I was putting my well-being first. Finally, I was taking responsibility for my life.

The first two years after leaving the marriage were very intense. I began to see myself in a new light, recognising for the first time the strong, attractive, talented and successful man in me. Seeing and accepting this was challenging. I was terrified people would think me egotistical and so reject me. I was poor at recognising my potential and achievements, finding it hard to accept praise or acknowledgement from others. I was also reluctant to give praise or acknowledgement to others. Slowly this was changing as I spent time reflecting on my past, spending time with those who loved me and treating myself in a more nurturing and appreciative manner.

At this time I was renting an apartment in Dublin and I began to pick up the pieces. I was lucky to have family and close friends around me who supported me. The first year living on my own was one of my best years in a long time. I took advantage of my newfound freedom, partying as much as possible, working less and having more sex than I had in the previous thirty-five years of my life. During this time I had relationships with two women in particular who impacted me for different reasons: Triona and Claire.

I was attracted to both women for seemingly different reasons. Triona was everything I had desired in a woman physically. She was tall, slim, very good looking, with long brown hair. She was eight years younger than me, which added to her appeal and she too was interested in all things spiritual and self-development related. She seemed like the perfect girlfriend for me. However, the relationship struggled from the very beginning and after two months we parted company.

Throughout this short relationship I was aware of thoughts such as, 'This is too good to be true; this won't last; what could she possibly see in me.' Just being in Triona's company brought up my insecurities. I constantly questioned if I was man enough to be with such a beautiful and loving woman. This relationship brought into plain view a strong pattern I had in relationships with women. I sabotaged my relationships due to self-limiting beliefs that I was not good enough and did not deserve the relationship.

This pattern made me needy and clingy, overly sensitive and paranoid. I needed to control situations and outcomes. I wanted others to suit me, to validate me. I depended on those close to me to provide me with the feeling of self-worth and acceptance. This insecurity was something I was slow to accept as part of myself, but I was very quick to judge it as wholly inappropriate in others.

Towards the end of the relationship with Triona we spent a week abroad. This was an intense experience for both of us. We both saw how we were being with each other. Living so closely together in a small space for a week meant there was no escaping the truth of our behaviours and attitudes. What I got was a snapshot of how I had behaved in my marriage: at times open and loving, but often distant, unpredictable, cold, judgemental, wanting sex without the emotional intimacy. On this holiday I had met myself.

Triona and I broke up after the holiday. We both needed to focus on resolving our own issues. I had to allow myself to feel everything, to be and feel alive without judging it or holding back. It took a while to let go of the relationship. I resisted being alone, I craved the physicality, the surface level relationship, feeling wanted and good enough without the intimate workout. The relationship had taught me much and if I could learn from the lessons then I might not repeat the same mistakes in future relationships.

I saw how controlling, pushy, demanding, and sexually obsessed I was. I had a tendency to be very resistant, closed and disconnected. I could be very intense, over analytical and unemotional. I also learned how much I enjoyed sex. I realised that I was physically attractive to some women, I had a kind, loving heart, and I could be vulnerable and loving when I relaxed and opened up.

I had spent much of the relationship with Triona telling her how she should be in it, how to open her heart and trust more. In reality I was actually talking to myself (not that I knew this at the time). I did not trust her or myself in the relationship to be present and open. Not committing meant not trusting.

I did not trust myself or even life itself. I believed that nothing good would happen to me, and if it did it would not last. I had little faith in the future. I dreamed about having a rich and abundant life with someone I loved and who loved me, but that was all I ever did – dream. My actions spoke a different truth. They demonstrated how I mistrusted life and had no faith in myself. I was all about control, fear management and a mentality of lack.

While I enjoyed living on my own I resisted being single, as I equated this with having no one and nothing in my life. This explains why I was slow to let things and people go. I needed to realise that being alone did not mean I could not have someone in my life. I could be alone without being lonely. What I needed to do was to focus inwards and feel my emotions, the grief of the marriage break-up, the pain and the loss. I needed to create space to mourn. Clinging to Triona was my way of avoiding all that. My holding on to her during and after the relationship was purely for my benefit, not hers. This was not love, just ego and it was aimed at meeting my selfish, insecure needs and desires.

This all began to slowly change in my relationship with Claire, whom I met some months after breaking up with Triona. Logically it should not have worked, as Claire was, in many ways, the opposite of Triona. Claire was almost the same age as me and small in stature. In the early days of this relationship I was aware of a voice in my head saying she was too small or the wrong age. She did not tick all the boxes on my ideal partner profile! In spite of this I felt drawn to her.

Thankfully I managed to ignore the superficial, egotistical way of viewing the opposite sex and relationships (in terms of a checklist). When Claire and I first started dating she had her own doubts about it because she was tired of casual relationships and wanted something more meaningful and serious. I on the other hand wanted a relationship with as little commitment as possible, or so I thought. After a couple of dates I decided it would be best if we stopped seeing each other as I believed I was not interested and should spend some time out on my own. Telling her this was easier than I had anticipated. The process of breaking up with Claire was, in hindsight, the reason we got back together.

It was a Monday morning in a Dublin café over breakfast where we said our final goodbyes. Over that meal we were present to each other in an intimate and loving manner. This happened organically. We were very open and real with each other. It felt safe to open up because there were no expectations from either of us. It was this experience that showed me that I could open my heart to another woman and feel love. This I realised several days after the event. In that breaking up I found and experienced what I had been looking for in all my other past relationships.

We both genuinely believed that that was it and we would at best remain friends. We walked away from each other that Monday morning letting go of any expectations of being together. In letting it go we were not trying to control or manipulate anything or anyone, we simply went on with life and trusted in things working out for each of us in the future. I was finally able and ready to be on my own; I was actually looking forward to it. I felt good about myself and was beginning to appreciate who I was and what I had. I was ready to be alone.

However, once I realised what had happened between us, how easily we had connected, I went back to Claire to see if she was interested in dating again. We agreed to take things slowly. The relationship grew from that moment on. It led to the birth of our son two years later. The love I have for both Claire and Josh, our son, is something I never thought possible and had almost given up on for myself in life.

So while in my head I had a clear image of the perfect woman for me, my heart had different ideas. When I finally stopped letting the head make all the decisions and put the heart in charge, everything changed for me. I found a woman I loved for who she was and she loved me for who I was. This only happened when I was ready to be real and open in the relationship on every level.

The relationship came back to us unexpectedly and in doing so, became a much richer and more meaningful experience for both of us. It can still be tough for both of us and takes work but it is a safe place to be ourselves. We have the capacity to spot each other's defences as they pop up and help each other through them. By being open, supportive and understanding with each other we are building our own esteem as well as that of the other partner and of our son.

⇥⟫⟫⟩⟨⟨⟨⟨⇤

There are other relationships that have proven to be equally as powerful in different ways, even though they were not romantic, such as those with neighbours, friends and work colleagues.

Throughout my working career I have worked alongside some very wise and impressive people. Adrian Mitchell, with whom I have spent eleven years working with as business partner and co-founder of the ILI, is one whom I was able to trust and be completely real with. Our working relationship enabled us to stay together for many years and to continue as close friends after I left the company. In fact leaving the company I set up with Adrian in 2003 was the second most difficult decision I had to make, after leaving my marriage.

In trying to decide whether to stay in the ILI or leave I consulted various people. I sought advice from friends, family, psychics, fortune tellers, astrologers, counsellors and healers. I wanted to be told what to do and be guaranteed success after doing it. All the different advice just added to my internal confusion and feeling of being stuck. Eventually it was such a distraction within me that I was becoming less present in my work and more of a hindrance to Adrian and the company. When I decided to leave it took me a few days to build up the courage to tell him, and even after telling him I still felt guilty, wishing things could be different and work out more cleanly for both of us. Not unlike during my marriage break-up, I wished we could stay and work together and continue to make the company a great success. He is an excellent teacher and one of the best coaches I know. Working with him I developed my own skills as a coach and a trainer and learned much in terms of self-awareness and self-development.

Of course I have learned much from relationships that were not so positive also.

Two in particular stand out. I had very different working relationships with both of them but the lessons I learned through my interactions with them were identical. Both relationships taught me about the importance of trusting myself.

I worked with both individuals at different points in my career. Both spoke with passion about living an authentic life and yet their actions contradicted this. I resented this and judged them as hypocrites. In both cases the relationship ended in acrimony. This reinforced my negative opinion of them and served to justify my own self-righteous views of how hypocritical they really were.

Ted was older than me and good at projecting an image of self-assuredness and maturity. He had been the driving force for the executive team we were both part of. He appeared very pragmatic, business-like and professional. At one of the team meetings he turned to me and said he did not trust me anymore and was not willing to work with me. I was stunned and felt a deep sense of disbelief and panic. The others jumped to my defence and he backed down. However, in the following months the relationships deteriorated. In a bid to take control of things and assert his authority Ted sought to take over the team. The rest of us were against this and after a protracted series of meetings and stand-offs he left.

I had to look at this experience in terms of my own learning. My emotional reaction in that meeting, where he told me he did not trust me, and immediately after it, indicated to me that I had trust issues. This did not excuse or justify Ted's behaviour. He behaved in typical bully style. It was vital to stand up to him and make it clear such behaviour was unacceptable. Personally, I needed to look inside and see what this was showing me. Over the subsequent weeks I reflected on the event and I saw through my actions and thoughts that I had no faith in myself to be successful in my work. I had no real confidence in my ability or potential.

Through honest reflection on my attitude and feelings, I saw how my sense of self-worth was externally driven. My sense of achievement and self-confidence was dependent on positive feedback from others. I was jealous of my colleagues when they received praise. I saw myself as being the weakest in the team. I feared not being taken seriously, of being challenged as to what I had to offer of value. I felt a fraud and was terrified of being found out.

This was a wake up call. I had to look at how I was relating to myself, how I saw myself and how much power I was giving away. Being told I was not trustworthy triggered feelings of panic, despair and emptiness, total rejection. I doubted everything about me – my abilities, my very purpose; it forced me to look at my rejection issues. The people-pleaser in me, the coward was calling the shots and in control. My heart was closed to me and to others. I trusted no-one, least of all myself and this was exactly what Ted, in retrospect, was showing me.

The second incident happened some years later. David and I worked together for a couple of years. In the beginning we got on well but there was something about him that bothered me. Aspects of his behaviour, his general attitude and his unpredictability made it difficult to fully trust him. I always felt that he was telling me distorted versions of the truth. He was prone to exaggerating and dramatising things. He was very intense and could never relax. He appeared to have boundless energy and nothing was too big or too risky for him.

Initially I was impressed by his energy and believed his talk about the possibilities for a great future. He said he would shake things up and transform how we worked. As time went on, he became more demanding, loud, arrogant, brash and hypersensitive. He showed no trust in others and in spite of his claims about what he could do he failed to deliver on his original commitments to the company. He was insecure, trying to be successful and desperately wanting to be liked by others but doing it in such an abusive way. It couldn't end any other way than in disappointment and bitter recriminations.

Looking back I could see how naïve I was. His lack of trust in others, particularly in me, reflected the lack of trust I had in myself. From our first meeting I was uncomfortable about working with him and yet I ignored this feeling. I let my head overrule my gut, telling myself that he was experienced. What he was telling me was exactly what we needed. I failed to trust my intuition and suffered the consequences.

## Starting again ... a little wiser, older and taking it like a man

Ever since being told I was adopted I wanted to meet my birth mother. The search began the year I was training as a teacher. I contacted an adoption society in Dublin. The search process was slow and frustrating. Five years later, in 1996, the agency came back telling me that my birth mother was ready to make contact. Initially this contact took the form of letters and photos. It was a surreal experience. I was living for the day when we would meet. That day came on the 30th January 1998. It was in the adoption agency building on Haddington Road. I walked up the stairs, led by the social worker, to the room where she was waiting.

After almost thirty years I was meeting my birth mother again. I felt a mix of conflicting emotions. As I entered the room she turned and walked towards me with a smile and open arms. We hugged. That first encounter was like meeting a close, old friend whom I had not seen for a long time. She did not feel like a stranger to me, even though I knew very little about her. We chain smoked our way through the meeting. Over the following year we met a number of times, slowly developing a bond.

I had found a piece of the jigsaw in my life. I had

a greater sense of my identity. The fact that my birth mother, Dolores, and I looked so alike helped me to feel I belonged somewhere. Seven months after our first meeting, Dolores arranged for me to meet her two daughters and son (I had already met her husband, John, by then). I was excited and terrified. A part of me feared that they might resent me turning up now and reject me. Still I was eager to meet them and hoped for a close relationship with each of them.

The meeting was in a hotel. I felt like a rubbery sponge, sweating and wobbling with nerves as I entered the hotel. But like most things in life it was not as bad as I had imagined. We chatted easily. Dermot, the youngest, cried because he was so happy to finally have a brother, or so he later told me. The two girls, Deirdre and Lisa, were easy to engage with. Lisa, the eldest, was chatty and outgoing. I was amazed by how similar we looked. I liked them a lot and was relieved that we easily connected.

Getting to know my birth family had its challenges. I share with one of my sisters a very similar temperament, which was great when we were in good moods. Like me she could be cutting and dismissive. I reacted to this by shutting down and pulling away from her. At times I felt uncomfortable around her and on my guard. As I became more aware of this I decided to address it. One day I seized the opportunity to talk to her in private. We spoke openly about our issues and realised both of us were feeling the same things about each other. Each of us was picking up on the other's unease and taking it personally. This clarity enabled us to be more relaxed together and to not prejudge the other.

A more alarming challenge greeted me with the other birth sister. This was a sexual attraction I felt towards her soon after our first meeting. I was confused and embarrassed about those feelings. I tried to ignore them. One night in the family house the two of us stayed up late drinking and chatting. I decided this was a good time to share my feelings for her. She was shocked by this revelation. She dismissed it as just a result of the confusing emotions I was feeling having just met this new family. I readily agreed and made light of my comments. However the feelings felt real and at the time I thought about what it would be like to have a relationship with her.

The next morning I was horrified at what I had said. I found it impossible to look my sister in the eye and could not get out of the house quick enough. Many years later I discovered that what I was experiencing was a recognised psychological effect of the reunion with a birth family. Reunions between birth relatives separated by adoption can spark off intense sexual feelings (according to Dr Maurice Greenburg, a consultant psychiatrist to London's Post-Adoption Centre). This phenomenon is called genetic sexual attraction (GSA). So what I had been experiencing all those years ago was common for people going through such an event.

The youngest in the birth family was my brother, Dermot, and for the first few years I had the least contact with him. I found it hard to connect with him, convincing myself that he found me dull and boring. We would chat about obvious things for a short while and then move on to our own individual activities. As he got older and I became more relaxed in myself our relationship developed and strengthened. But convincing myself that I was relevant in his life was a challenge for me.

While I was thrilled to have my birth family, their arrival into my life threw a world of new challenges at me. Going through these challenges helped me to uncover my blind spots and pockets of self-denial. They helped me to open my heart, to love and express myself more. I became more grounded and present with them. It is wonderful to have two mothers and I feel very close to both of them. They each bring something unique and rich into my life. While the bond I have with Dolores runs deep, it is Patricia, my adoptive mother, who will always be my Mam.

The lack of father figures in my life was compensated for by the presence of the maternal figures to some extent. With the arrival of my son I was forced to face the one issue that I had avoided for almost forty years. Becoming a father had awakened the Man in me.

My life, personally and professionally, has always been full of women. I always felt drawn to them and preferred their company. Growing up I regularly played with my sister's girlfriends and connected more easily with my female cousins. My mother had one brother (a second brother had died when she was young) and four sisters and Dad had two sisters. So the family was predominantly female. My birth mother has three sisters and one brother, who died of alcoholism a year after I first met him.

Father figures have eluded me for much of my life. My birth father disappeared before I was born. After my adoptive father died the only close male in my life was an adoptive relative from the UK, Pat. He was a big, gentle man, whom I got on well with the few times we met. It was after his sudden death in 1997 that I realised how much I cared for him. I had replaced Dad with Pat. I never cried so much as I did the night I got the news of Pat's death. The tears came from the depths of my being. All I wanted was to be left alone to cry my heart out. A month earlier we had spoken on the phone and agreed I would go visit him soon. I kept procrastinating on this visit, letting work distract me. In the end I did visit, to attend his funeral.

Later my father in law began to fill the void left by Pat's death. We enjoyed each other's company at the weekends. One night after a long drinking session I told him how much he meant to me as a father figure. Given that he had his head in the kitchen sink making retching noises as I was telling him this, it is unlikely he got the message. Our relationship ended when my marriage to his daughter ended. Once again I was fatherless.

The absence of a father figure in my early adult life

left its mark. Male energy is about action, achievement, strength and physical assertion. I had diluted these with fear, hesitancy and self-doubt. Unconsciously I attempted to fill this gap through forming professional working relationships with older men. I wanted to be successful but was unwilling to do this on my own. I never felt man enough. The alpha male inside me was ignored and distrusted.

This rejection of my maleness coloured my attitude to men. Some I admired for their pro-active and courageous acts, others I pilloried for their perceived faults. My birth father, whom I have not met, was someone I judged as weak and a coward for abandoning my birth mother. My thinking was black and white on such issues and given my history with fathers it was no wonder I had my own father issues to deal with.

For as long as possible I avoided fatherhood. I never felt ready. I told myself kids are too much hassle, too expensive, too demanding, or simply not for me. The idea of being a father scared me. I saw children as too much responsibility. For a brief period while I was married I did want a child. However, at this stage cracks were appearing in the relationship and we agreed that to have a child at that time would be for the wrong reasons. We needed to sort ourselves out first before we brought a third party to the table. When the marriage ended I gave up on the idea of having children. I had accepted that I would be at most an uncle. However, life had other plans for me. Two and a half years after leaving the marriage, I unexpectedly became a father.

The night Claire told me she was pregnant I was sitting on the couch watching TV oblivious to the new life that was now in the room. When she said she was pregnant I instantly broke into a cold sweat and panic flashed up inside me. Almost as quick I pulled back from the panic and focused on Claire who looked just as shocked and scared. I tried to lighten the moment for both of us. As I did a feeling of wanting to protect her and our child, a primal instinct which I had never felt before, burst open inside me. This motivated me to embrace our new reality as parents.

Questions such as: was I proud to be a father? Did I feel good enough or competent to be a dad? How was I a father to me? became dominant in my mind. I began to think deeply about fatherhood and what it actually meant to me. It was a daunting responsibility but also an amazing gift. Deep down I knew I could be a fantastic father. I believed that by loving our child, I was loving me, the two were inseparable. This was one sure way of being alive and present.

Once Josh was born any tendency I had towards self-absorption weakened. I could not stay ruminating on personal insights and philosophical concepts with Josh babbling and grinning at me. Josh, unplanned and unasked for, turned out to be the key to opening my heart. The love I feel for Josh is deep, unconditional, primal and intense. In his presence I can became softer, calmer and more loving. The best and, sometimes, the worst in me – the intolerant, judgemental bully – are brought out effortlessly. I feel like a man, a father and a dad with him. I have more fun because of Josh. I act the fool and he loves it.

I am more aware of the choices and decisions I make now. The future I create is also for him. I love his company and want to see him growing up and spot the subtle changes that only a loving parent will see. I want him to be proud of me and to love me. Therefore, I must put the appropriate foundations in for this to happen. I can love Josh and be with him in ways that my birth father and adoptive father were not. Both men taught me much through their presence and absence. I can refuse to let my insecurities hold me back from being the best father I can be.

Being a father holds considerable responsibilities and incredible rewards. It challenges me to face my fears and self-limiting beliefs. The old patterns and limiting beliefs must end with me and not be passed on to my son. The choices I make in each moment are what matter. Change comes through new choices. These choices must come from the heart. The heart is my only choice point. Real choices, which is my real power, only happen when I am in my heart. Within the first year of his life, Josh taught me so much about living and loving. He taught me more than all my years of researching and study, simply because he got me to live it.

Before Josh arrived I felt more like a teenager or an immature adult, waiting to grow up. I did not feel ready to stand on my own two feet in the world. I felt inadequate and weak, which made life very stressful. I compared myself to others in relation to work, attractiveness, achievement and I always came out the worst. I was my own worst critic. This attitude reinforced my feelings of inadequacy. My inner critic held me back from taking risks and speaking up. It caused me to doubt my own decisions and not trust my gut. It robbed me of self-belief.

In my teaching, career guidance and coaching work there was always an underlying sense that I lacked something. I rarely challenged this feeling, accepting it at face value. Through raising my self-awareness and examining my past, I had begun to see how false this attitude was. I had been living a lie for too long.

My ability to limit myself was formidable. In spite of this I had managed to gain some level of success in my life. I wondered what I could achieve in the next forty years of my life using all my resources free from the limiting beliefs. Being aware of how I limited myself in the past enabled me to make new decisions. I could challenge the negative thoughts as soon as they popped into my awareness. I began taking back control of me.

This transformation coincided with the break-up of my marriage and my physical awakening. The inner changes I was waking up to, in terms of my own self-worth and well-being, were manifesting externally. I started taking salsa dance classes and discovered I had hips! Once I got over the initial embarrassment of gyrating in public I started to enjoy the dancing. I began dating women. I changed my hairstyle and wardrobe. In fact the only thing I did not change was my sex.

My work was mirroring me back to myself throughout this whole process. Clients were coming for coaching on very similar personal issues and seeking to overcome their own fears, inner critics and self-limiting beliefs. The work I needed to do for myself was the very work I found myself doing with clients. This change, which began when I acknowledged my repressed emotions and fears, was coming full circle.

The closing of this circle and this period of my life was signified by my new roles as father and partner at the age of forty. I wondered was this a mid-life crisis. I remember listening to a man being interviewed on radio about a serious personal health trauma. His story was about recovery and new beginnings. He was diagnosed at forty years of age with head and neck cancer and was not expected to live. He survived twelve hours of surgery. His recovery was slow, with setbacks including contracting meningitis twice. He was a runner and his history of running gave him the attitude to keep going, just to the next turn or bend, keep moving forward bit by bit.

Today he is healthy, in a new career and living his life with "pleasant recklessness". By this he means that he has an attitude to life now quite different to before his illness, he does things differently, is more spontaneous and less risk averse; he enjoys the moment and takes far less for granted. He appreciates what he has and engages fully with life. It was a fascinating and inspiring story, and it all began at the age of forty.

Another example was Michael. He was a student on one of my coaching courses. He was a father of two and fifty-three years old. He was a priest for fifteen years and at the age of forty he gave up that life and started a new one as a trainer, husband and father. There are many examples of people who made significant life changes at forty. I wondered was I experiencing all of this because I was coming up to forty. Maybe it was a point in one's life when things naturally came to the surface for resolution. In the world of shamanism for example, forty is a significant time for change and transition, however, a minor one compared to the seismic shift that supposedly occurs at fifty.

Mid-life crisis or not, I had begun a new life. Without any clear plan or intention to do so, I found myself in a new relationship and I had a son. I appeared to be moving into a new career in personal development through writing and speaking, which had always been my ambition. I was reconnecting with my spirituality. Life was happening without huge effort on my part, I more willingly went with its flow.

## So that's why I loved The Exorcist!

In 2008 something happened that convinced me I had found the root cause of all my problems. A Catholic priest who was also a psychotherapist was recommended to me by two different people. Out of curiosity to see what was so great about him and an urge in me to get clarity around leaving the ILI I booked a session. We discussed my adoption, my marriage break-up, my varied career, and the persistent sense of emptiness in me.

Halfway through the session he asked, 'So what do you think is the root cause of all your pain?' I thought about this and said, 'Probably the fact that I was adopted, that I was actually abandoned at birth.' His reply was, 'That's not it; it is earlier than that.' I thought some more and tentatively said, 'It must have been due to the horrible feelings and emotions I felt living in the womb of my birth mother.' His reply again was, 'No, that is not it.' That surprised me and my next thought was, 'bloody hell, please don't tell me this is due to some past life stuff.' Having worked on plenty of past life stuff before I saw no solution in that. He asked me, 'Are you ready to hear this? Do you want to know the real cause?' I looked at him and firmly said, 'Yes'.

He said, 'You are a womb-twin survivor. You had a twin in the womb who died.' This shocked me. I had never heard of this before. At the same time what I was hearing actually felt familiar. Of course I had no proof but as we talked about it and he brought me through a questionnaire, based on the symptoms and characteristics of womb-twin survivors, I appeared to be a textbook example.

Apparently the loss of my twin in the womb had a severe energetic and psychological impact on me and since then I was living life in a post-traumatic stress state. This seemed bizarre but I was relieved that I had possibly reached the beginning of the end of my pain.

He suggested that I give my twin a name. I called him John.

I left feeling a mixture of hope and doubt. Over the following weeks a number of incidents occurred which served to reinforce the womb-twin theory in my life. One event in particular stood out as more than coincidence and resulted in me accepting the story as fact in my life.

I ordered a book on womb-twin survivors. Instead of having it posted to me I decided to call into the shop to collect it, something I rarely did. The sales guy who served me suggested I get another book on the same topic. It turned out that he too was a womb-twin survivor. We chatted for some time and as I was about to leave I felt compelled to ask him his name. It was Ian John. I was stunned. My name (I am often called Ian by those unfamiliar with the spelling for Eoin) and my twin's name combined. I left the store believing my womb-twin story.

This womb-twin or vanishing twin phenomenon is quite common. Elizabeth Noble in *Primal Connections* says that it is well known that more twins are conceived than born. In the past few years, anecdotal, yet interesting, research has been carried out in this area by Althea Hayton of www.wombtwin.com. Through her work a list of characteristic statements, related to particular attitudes, behaviours, feelings and relationships, were gradually pieced together from stories told by womb-twin survivors. This combined with a list of signs and indicators of a twin pregnancy that ended with a sole survivor, formed the basis of a comprehensive research questionnaire which can be completed online to discover if one might be a womb twin survivor. Full details on this and related information are available on www.wombtwin.com.

Many of the psychological and emotional characteristics listed in this research jumped out at me as strong patterns and experiences in my own life. In fact I quickly realised I had the majority of them. Fear of abandonment, a deep sense of loneliness, fear of rejection, a constant feeling that something was missing from my life, constant searching but not sure for what exactly, a strong feeling of being different from others and of not being able or willing to fit in, a persistent sense of not reaching my potential were just a small sample of the characteristics of a womb-twin survivor.

Who could have predicted this outcome? All my seeking had culminated in being told I was a womb-twin survivor. This was akin to a dodgy, desperate plot line of a TV soap trying hard to boost ratings. The psychotherapist also told me that my twin continued to live through me, was draining me and causing me to feel confused about who I was and what I wanted to do. Needless to say this freaked me. Memories of old science fiction movies and trashy horror movies about demonic possessions came to mind. So life really was stranger than fiction. It appeared to explain so much: how I limited myself, why I was so fearful, negative and self-critical, why I felt alone and like an outsider for so long. It explained why I always felt I deserved nothing good in life and that ultimately I did not deserve to exist.

While this promised to be the final missing piece of the puzzle of understanding Me, it was really just another twist in my lifelong pattern of seeking. Eventually I would realise that as intriguing as this new information was to me, I still had to live my life and decide to either embrace a new future free from my old patterns or continue to repeat the past by allowing such patterns to dictate the outcomes of my experiences.

Knowledge and information, like awareness, are important but only to the extent that they are applied in the decisions and choices we make. Reflecting on my life in detail, I spotted several strong patterns that needed to be challenged if I was to break free from my fears, insecurities and self-sabotaging behaviours. A process of change began in earnest and through it I learned some simple, obvious and essential life lessons.

# **Section** TWO

Behind the Story
The Process: Finding Patterns
and Learning Lessons

So that's my story, or the highlights at least. It has its share of pain, confusion, regret, success and happiness, and like anyone's story it is full of noise and drama. However, our stories are a distraction from the real information. Our stories are just a gathering of events and experiences that we identify with. Focusing on or getting caught up in this drama is pointless. The story is only the beginning, a starting point for unpacking the real information.

The real information, which is buried beneath all the drama, is the life lessons and insights we need to learn. We can use this information to create a more harmonious and easier life. All the answers we seek to life's challenges and problems are stuffed in the cracks and corners of the story and can be easily seen if we remember that the story is just the surface detail, the vehicle for the real information. These lessons are easy to miss if we believe that the story is the most important thing about us. Look past the story – no one is their story.

So let me unpack my drama of some of its feedback and insights. With any story there are dominant patterns of behaviour and thinking which create predictable results. Within these patterns are important lessons that will enable us to make real change, transforming the patterns and the results we get in life. A summary of the process is provided in Box 2a.

## Hidden in the open – spotting patterns

I did not set out in the beginning to look for patterns in my life. I was not even aware of such things. All I wanted was to understand why I was so full of fear and pain. I worked on improving my self-awareness and through this process patterns began to emerge. This work started by turning my attention and focus inwards. Working from the inside out enabled me to experience clarity, calmness, humility, and compassion. Slowly patterns appeared from where they had always been, right in front of me in the everyday detail of my life. No big drama or long cathartic process was necessary to discover these patterns. All that was required was a desire to know and the openness to see them.

### THE PROCESS

Self-acceptance is found through understanding the self. Understanding the self requires awareness and a desire for insight. This gives rise to the process of self-acceptance or opening up which involves the following :

- Be present, observe the self non-judgementally
- Note your reactions, choices, behaviours and dominant thoughts
- Reflect on what has been observed
- Be open to feedback on your behaviours, attitudes etc. from trusted others, through journaling, personal encounters and other everyday life events
- Identify patterns of behaviours/thinking/reactions across what may appear to be different events or experiences
- Focus on an instance where a pattern occurs and explore the underlying dynamics by asking yourself some of the following questions:

    - What exactly is happening here?
    - What exactly am I thinking?
    - What exactly am I feeling?
    - What do I believe about this situation?
    - What buttons are being pushed inside me in this situation?
    - What is all this telling me about myself?
    - Where and/or when have I reacted like this before?

- The next time the pattern shows up, respond differently and break the pattern. With awareness you can choose a new way of responding in that situation, rather than just reacting from habit.

In choosing a new response, ensure it is from the heart and make this way of being and responding a new pattern. Only in this way will you consistently experience more desirable and positive outcomes.

– Box 2a –

The best-self help course available to us all is life itself and the best teacher we can learn from is the person we are with in each moment. All insights and lessons about who we are and how we can heal are forever coming at us through the everyday encounters in ordinary living. We just have to pay close attention.

The truth of who we are is always staring us in the face. It is hidden in the open, amongst the people and places that fill our lives. There are no real mysteries here; it is our head that complicates these issues through excessive analysis and intellectualising what only ever needs to be witnessed, acknowledged and embraced. Thinking is a very small part of the overall process.

When we relax and open up to life in each moment, then we are engaging with life in a more meaningful way. When I began to lighten up and stopped being so self-critical I was able to appreciate the learning and insights that life had to offer me each day. I quickly began to see how strongly patterned my life really was. I was operating on auto-pilot. I was, in the words of Anthony de Mello, walking through life asleep. Every pattern I discovered was an opportunity to reclaim my power, through raising my self-awareness and providing myself with the capacity to make decisions and choices consciously. Discovering my patterns became easier as I slowed down. The most effective method I found for doing this was meditation.

I meditated sitting in a comfortable position for a minimum of twenty minutes twice a day, once in the morning and again in the evening. Some days I might only manage one meditation session, but I made it a priority that each day had some level of meditation in it. I meditated using a mantra which I was given in my training in primordial sound meditation. There are many different ways to meditate and it is worth trying a number of different types until you hit on the method that suits you best and allows you to experience the incredible psychological, physiological and emotional benefits of regular meditation.

Through meditation I discovered my inner world. It quickly raised my self-awareness. I discovered feelings of great discomfort in the beginning. Sometimes the urge to stop meditating and do something, anything, to escape from these feelings was overwhelming. As I persisted with meditation, deeper feelings of fear, inadequacy and unworthiness surfaced. On days when such feelings were persistently present all I wanted to do was stay in bed or get drunk.

Through meditation I discovered a limiting belief which coloured my thinking and was at the root of many of my dysfunctional patterns. I believed I was a mistake. I saw myself as a misfit, an outsider, in the way, not meant to be here, and felt I should keep my head down, stay hiding, not be found out, that I had no right to exist, that I had nothing to offer because I was not meant to be. I lived my life at a subsistence level, doing enough to get by. I was the reluctant substitute hoping not to be called onto the pitch to play his part in the game of life.

As I continued to meditate I saw how these feelings

blocked me from achieving my goals. Whenever I visualised my goals, thoughts such as 'too good to be true; I don't deserve it; I am not good enough' came bursting up. This was the sabotaging script I had been living with all these years.

Meditation proved to be a powerful method of discovering my truth. Through this process of spending time with myself I was facing repressed emotions. Regularly meditating helped me to declutter my mind and my world around me. As I slowed down I became calmer, which brought greater clarity. I was witnessing patterns in my day-to-day life. I saw how I was reacting to events and people, the choices I was making and the reality I was creating for myself. For the first time I was aware of the part I played in creating my life. I saw where my responsibility was and always had been. I was finally meeting and getting to know the real me, warts and all.

In the next section I have summarised my dominant patterns of behaviour and thinking under three main types. While they may be familiar to most people, personal examples are included to show how subtle and prevalent these patterns can be.

## This patterned life

### Lack of abundance or an abundance of lack?

The attitude of lack or not enough felt normal to me as a way of thinking. It operated below my radar of awareness, controlling my decisions and behaviours. It touched every part of my life. I bought online products on abundance and financial freedom, yet would never follow through on them. I regularly felt that there was not enough time to get all I wanted done in a day. I would get frustrated by my perceived lack of progress in a task. I habitually focused on what was missing, absent and wrong. A sense that I was lacking in knowledge, qualifications or experience dominated my early career.

My lack mentality caused me to take refuge in the pursuit of knowledge. I overemphasised the importance of the academic side of life as a means of feeling good enough. I attached my sense of self-esteem to this. Not long after I completed my Masters I considered applying for a PhD. The title Doctor appealed to me, I believed I would then be the expert, that people would respect me and look up to me. I would be good enough. Thanks to my coaching course I spotted this flawed thinking before taking any action. I would have been doing a PhD for all the wrong reasons. Such short-sighted ineffective decision-making was inevitable when my self-esteem was rooted in things and people outside of myself. My self-esteem was buried in academic success.

I habitually gathered and held on to information. I

would gather too much information for a project, which slowed progress. When marketing seminars and courses I would worry about how many people would turn up. Feelings of inadequacy such as, not experienced enough, not fit enough, not good looking enough, not intelligent or articulate enough, were common. I hoarded. I hated throwing things like books, toys and clothes away. Every piece of food had to be used in some way in the house. Food on my plate had to be finished, rather than thrown out.

Having one of anything was rarely enough. When I took up photography I bought three SLR cameras. I could have easily managed on one and certainly two were all I ever needed. I excelled at focusing on what was wrong or missing, which served to keep me stuck in life. I found it hard to let go of people and things. I lacked self-confidence. Anything that seemed risky was avoided. The fear of failure and rejection was too strong. When I considered learning a new skill such as speaking Italian for example, my immediate thoughts focused on the commitment involved, the length of time it would take to get to an acceptable skill level. Thoughts such as 'I can't do it; it's too much effort; there is no point; I won't succeed' swirled inside my head. I felt demotivated by the idea of such effort. I wanted the success but without the effort. I was unwilling to commit to the challenge.

Fear of not having enough money always haunted me. The negative patterns played out most clearly in my relationship with money. I never felt I had enough. Even when I had a substantial amount, I managed to end up losing the bulk of it through legal bills and poor investment decisions. I did not feel good enough to earn loads of money. I seemed to be obsessed about money. Even when I was a kid I regularly stole money at home. Asking people to pay for my services and setting appropriate fees challenged me. Feeling rich was alien to me. (I took for granted my health, my academic and career success, my intellect and my ability to make friends, the love I received from family, partners and friends.) With such a lack of gratitude for the bounty already in my life, it was no wonder feeling abundant was strange.

Uprooting old limiting beliefs around money was necessary. Educating myself on how money worked was essential. The simple and obvious advice in Robert Parsons' book *The Money Secret* is that to create financial wealth you need to spend less than you earn. This was easy for me to dismiss. At the same time I was ignoring the fact that if I failed to apply it then I would always be financially poor.

Chronic dissatisfaction may not be an illness or an official psychological disorder but it was a strong feature of my lack mentality. In the back of my mind was the nagging sense that somewhere out there was something better. This could be a better job, a better house, a better partner or a better life. This feeling of being vaguely and constantly dissatisfied with my lot was linked to the proverbial habit of thinking that the grass is greener next door. Very often the greener grass next door was another woman.

In 2007 I decided to escape to Vietnam for a few months to attend a self-awareness retreat. I needed space to decide on my future in the ILI. I was also looking to have fun and maybe even find myself in the process. I failed to find myself but I loved Vietnam. The workshop focused on enhancing awareness and presence, providing a rare opportunity to slow down. I played volleyball, swam, did yoga and received massages regularly. Gradually I noticed how I reacted to my environment. One pattern in particular showed up through my interactions with a woman in the workshop. I was attracted to her. I fantasised about being in a relationship with her. Somehow I noticed what I was doing. I was focusing on this girl, wondering what it would be like to be with her. It hit me that this was what I habitually did. I was looking for someone better than the girl I was already in a relationship with. I was not content. Seeing this, I now had a choice. I could continue to pursue this woman or commit to my current partner and let the pattern go. I picked the latter option by telling the girl about my new relationship, the pattern soon fell away and I enjoyed the rest of my time in Vietnam conflict free.

All-or-nothing thinking was part of this pattern. The way to change this thinking was to look for some form of balance in what I did. Living by extremes was never healthy and not sustainable. The antidote to this attitude of lack was an attitude of gratitude. This changed the focus and intention behind my actions and thoughts. I began to practise appreciating what I already had and celebrating the abundant life I currently enjoyed. I kept a daily gratitude log. This began a slow turnaround from my attachment to lack towards abundance, appreciation and being good enough.

Letting go of the pattern is a moment-to-moment experience and requires persistence in the beginning to overcome the normal resistance to change. Eventually, like everything in life, when I stop paying it attention it starts to fade away.

## Keeping control, at all costs

A certain amount of control in our lives is important. Too often we try to control due to fear and resistance. I habitually chose to control rather than relax and go with the flow. The need for control was driven by a desire to feel safe. It was very stressful and tiring trying to exert and maintain control all the time. It dominated behaviours and interactions with others as I grew up. Living in the head as opposed to the whole body reinforced this. Over-analysis kept me rooted in my head from where I judged the world as unsafe. Spontaneity was not an option. The control freak in me indulged in excessive scheduling, creating numerous to-do lists on scraps of paper. I had to know what was planned for the weekend days in advance. When travelling in the car I preferred to be the driver, a very impatient driver. I avoided activities such as dancing and team sports as they required me to be in the body. The fact that I negatively judged controlling behaviours in others was a clear indication of my own control issues.

Passion in life is quality not quantity and I had ignored this. I lived life in two dimensions only. In order to feel safe I repressed much of my potential and passion for life and accepted being just a shadow of myself. To express myself creatively and passionately felt risky and scary. This protective and controlled way of living lasted until my mid-thirties.

My ability to control my emotions was depressingly impressive. To feel emotions required letting go and being present in the body. Instead, I adopted strategies to suppress or distract from my emotions throughout my youth such as setting fires, hoarding and comfort eating. Later, I found refuge in the academic arena where cognitive skills were greatly valued, and this allowed me to remain head focused. Inevitably, things changed when I entered the world of work. This move was equivalent to my leaving the classroom and stepping onto the sports field at school. I was stepping out of my bubble of security and into a place of unknown risks and fears. It was in the world of work that I discovered how emotionally repressed I was. Sooner or later I would have to accept the importance of feeling and expressing my emotions appropriately. It would take a lot of painful soul searching, the death of a loved one and a marriage break-up to get me to feel fully.

The constant need to know in advance how things would turn out made it hard to focus on the now. Constantly being future focused in a fearful way often sabotaged the very thing I desired. For example while I made the decision initially to leave my company in 2006, it was not until 2011 that I actually took action and left. In the intervening years I hovered back and forth between being determined to leave and terrified of being out on my own. I sought advice from family, friends, and work colleagues as to what I should do and wanted them to tell me that if I left, it would be the right decision and a great success. I felt I needed this reassurance before I could leave. I had no faith in my own judgement. Needing the reassurance of a positive outcome before I took the first step was a recipe for procrastination, which I practised for five years.

I always struggled with process. Be it the major stuff such as grieving fully for my dad's death, to the minor stuff like reading a detailed document or article for work. I preferred to cut through the detail and reach the end point quickly. I preferred the big picture. Feeling certain emotions and processing them was something I resisted for many years. This impacted my goal setting. Being focused only on the end result meant that the process, the creative part and the only part I have any control of, suffered from micro-management. Instead of trying to manipulate, avoid or fast-track the process, it needed to be my focus, rather than the outcome. By investing my time and energy in the process I was optimising my chances of a successful outcome. For me the process was outside of my comfort zone. It required me to be present, attend to detail, feel, as well as think and trust in my ability to achieve the outcome as I engaged in the process. I needed to stop resisting the process. Life was about process and to minimise it in any way was trying to fight my very nature, which was life itself. There is nothing more frustrating and destructive than resisting the natural flow or process of life. Yet this was what I was consistently doing – resisting the inevitable, trying to stay in the comfort bubble I had created.

The impact of the control pattern was very evident in my relationships. Instead of loving I was simply controlling. Real love means allowing the other person to be who they want to be and if that includes letting them go their own way, then so be it. If we are right together or meant to be together then that will be the case so long as I trust and not try to control or influence the outcome. In my relationship with Triona, and with Laura, I was trying to manage them to make things work. Manipulating and bullying in subtle forms were part of this pattern. This created stress and was a major reason for the relationships ending. In relationships, I was forever trying to figure out what others thought of me, because their opinions mattered so much and I was addicted to their approval. Connecting with others meant being vulnerable and possibly getting hurt. In my youth the appeal of the religious life highlighted my fear of connecting with others. Eventually I connected with Claire. The control pattern weakened as a result, which served to strengthen the relationship further.

My year spent in the agricultural college being miserable and feeling sorry for myself was a result of living too much in my head and resisting everything about the experience. I was simply not present. The year could not go fast enough and my eagerness to speed up time added to my unhappiness. With greater awareness I could have accepted my environment. In doing so I would have been taking back control, rather than simply reacting and wanting things to change. If I could go back in time to that year and briefly chat to my younger self I would tell him to lighten up and accept the situation. My attitude to the situation was entirely within my control. Instead of focusing on what was wrong, I could have focused on more positive aspects of the experience. That year demonstrated how I create my own misery when I resist or fight against the reality of a situation.

The stronger the resistance, the greater the potential rewards that await you if you go through that resistance. One example of this was well illustrated by Chuck Yeager. He was the first pilot in the world to fly faster than the speed of sound. In 1947 he was assigned to test the rocket-powered X-1 fighter plane. No one knew if a fixed-wing aircraft could fly faster than sound, or if a human pilot could survive the experience. Scientists and engineers at that time believed flying at or close to the speed of sound was suicide. Previous attempts to fly faster than sound had failed due to the fact that the plane would begin to shake violently as it came closer to this speed and the pilot read this as a signal to slow down believing the plane was about to disintegrate. Chuck Yeager viewed this shaking differently. He saw it as resistance from the plane approaching the sound barrier. The shaking was simply a reflection of the degree of resistance being experienced by the aircraft. Such strong resistance told him he was close to his target speed, and was a signal to him to persist. Seconds later he broke through the resistance and the sound barrier. In recognising the resistance for what it was, he knew what to do and consequently it is his name that is lauded in the annals of aviation history.

Feeling resistance to anything is a sign to pay more attention to that which you are resisting. I began to listen to my resistance. As I listened I saw that the resistance was fear and negative thinking. Like an old coat that I still wore even though it was torn and too small for me, I had outgrown it but was reluctant to throw it away because it was so familiar. The resistance came from the insecure part of me that wanted things to stay the same. This of course was not possible. So now I feel the resistance and do it anyway. That is the only way I can be free of it. Resistance is a positive sign that I am moving in the right direction and the key is to move into and through the resistance.

Resistance feels different and serves a very different purpose to gut feeling or intuition. Intuition is feedback at a body level, which is about having a sense that something such as a course of action or decision is right or wrong without knowing why. For example, the day I decided to leave my marriage I knew in my gut it was the right thing to do. But soon after the decision I began to question myself and analyse my intuition. This created resistance to the decision to leave. The resistance was all about the fear, the possible horrible consequences of leaving. The resistance was trying to convince me to stay, where it was familiar and safe. Eventually I walked through my resistance and left. Waiting on the other side of that resistance was a whole new life.

Instead of habitually controlling I needed to relax and trust more. I could achieve this by allowing myself to feel more deeply more often. I wanted to feel fully and live fully, experience the passion of life. I had to be willing to embrace situations and people around whom I felt uncomfortable and allow this feeling to be, rather than avoid them and miss potential opportunities for growth and success. I had to accept life as my teacher, open up to my experiences and trust in the process of life. Only in this way would I be able to clear out my toxic emotional clutter.

Self-control is essential and it involves control of my responses to my inner and outer worlds. All I ever have control of is my response, my attitude to what is or is not happening.

## Hiding behind my cynic

A cynic is a pessimist, a sneer, distrustful and suspicious. I came to recognise it as a very strong mindset that dominated my thinking, and therefore my life. Cynicism as a pattern was fundamental to the survival of the other patterns. And like the other patterns it was driven by fear. It was through this cynical attitude that I perceived myself and my potential. I found it very hard to spot my strengths and successes. My opinion of Me was lower than anyone else's opinion of me could ever be. My judgements of myself served to shut me down and frequently kept me from sharing my talents and gifts with others. It stopped me from pursuing my passions, paralysing me through over-analysing. I was a complete bastard towards myself, judging myself harshly at every opportunity. Nothing I did was good enough. Sarcasm also featured. As a young teacher I used sarcasm as a defence against feelings of inadequacy. Cynicism was a defence against feeling a failure, being rejected or judged harshly by others. It worked by keeping a distance between me and others. The cynic was my front man, my mask to hide behind.

Luke was a friend who was very successful in business. He had made substantial amounts of money through a number of different enterprises. I admired his entrepreneurial spirit and ability to take risks. I even envied his success. When we spoke I always asked him how his businesses were going. As I asked him I was aware of the cynic in me hoping to hear him say things were not going well, he had lost money or screwed up in some way. The cynic in me wanted him to fail so that I could feel OK about my inaction on certain projects. This would allow me to stay in my miserable comfort zone of inaction and "safe" living.

I detested cynicism in others. The negative experiences with my old work colleagues, David and Ted, clearly taught me this. Both men were in their own ways very cynical in how they manipulated and sought to control people and events around them. Through my own cynicism I got pulled into their game. It taught me the importance of integrity, in other words doing what I said I would do and only saying what I actually meant. I needed to stop putting others, including myself, on a pedestal as this only served to perpetuate the cycle of separation, disappointment and frustration I experienced in relationships. I needed to trust myself first and to stop looking to others to sort my own stuff out. The challenge was to stand up and lead myself. The incidents around trust with Ted and David highlighted this for me. Like them I had been preaching one message and practising the opposite. Painful as they were, these incidents threw me into a more powerful space within myself. I ceased being a victim.

I was too good at avoiding feeling and could see how this played out in many areas of my life. While holidaying in Donegal one summer with Claire, we visited an elderly couple she knew. Here I witnessed how I denied my own emotions. Immediately prior to and during the visit I was feeling uncomfortable. During the visit I noticed how I was judging myself through the elderly couple's eyes. A part of me felt guilt and shame over my broken marriage and over being a separated man with Claire. I felt the elderly couple were judging me when really it was me judging myself. This was the source of my discomfort, which had nothing to do with the elderly couple. Later I realised that I had rarely allowed myself to feel guilt and shame as I judged these feelings to be beneath me, telling myself, 'I am better than that or, I should know better than to feel guilt or worry.' I was not allowing myself to be human, to emotionally connect. I was shutting myself down through my self-judgements and projecting them onto others to make them credible.

Another aspect of this was how I judged those who expressed strong emotions of any type. I always struggled with letting myself cry. I rarely allowed myself to express or feel anger. Even my son, Josh, was teaching me how to handle emotions. In his first six months of life I noticed how uncomfortable I felt when he started crying. I usually pulled back from comforting him. I would become distant and cold, impatient and intolerant. I shut my heart to him in those moments, judging his crying as petty. I realised that this was also what I did to myself, which stopped me from feeling the pain that I carried and which held me back from being creative, expressive and joyful.

In some cases I overcame my fears and harsh self-judgements. For example, I joined a local toastmasters' club in 2004. Toastmasters International is a non-profit educational organisation that operates clubs worldwide for the purpose of helping members improve their communication, public speaking and leadership skills. Two years after joining I had made it to the district (UK and Ireland) finals competition, where the winner would go on to represent the UK and Ireland at the World Toastmasters competition in Washington DC. Getting to the district finals was the result of going with the flow. I was not trying to win. I just accepted the opportunity to speak and enjoyed the experience of competing at each stage. By not taking the competition and myself too seriously I was able to relax and enjoy my progress.

Sometimes the cynic was so strong that it had me doing things that seemed ridiculous. At times I had all the signs of being a social phobic. One aspect of Toastmasters that I always found difficult was making myself attend a meeting. Once in the meeting I was fine; thinking about going was the problem. This was true for most public events I was attending. Feelings of inadequacy and fears of rejection arose from thinking about going. I had no evidence or logical reason to feel this way. But what I feel inside is my reality, as it is what I experience and determines how I behave. Given the choice I would stay indoors, hiding away, just like when I was happy sitting in the cardboard box.

One day I got a phonecall from a woman enquiring about my lifecoaching service. It was in the early days of building my practice. She explained how her life was controlled by an overwhelming fear of leaving her home. She feared meeting people, convinced they would judge her harshly. She knew how harmful this fear was for her and was hoping coaching could help. Soon after this call I realised the woman was describing exactly how I felt. I was stunned when I realised her experience was the very same as mine. She was a mirror for me to see how I avoided meeting people. When I did meet people I judged myself negatively, convinced that people were not interested in me. This negative thinking was an unconscious strategy to keep me from engaging with others and avoid rejection. If I rejected them first, at least in my head, then they could not reject me.

I never considered myself to be a quitter but every time I let the inner judge control my actions and attitude, I became one. I loved the sound and the feel of the saxophone. I spent a year taking saxophone lessons and then quit. What made me quit was the constant nagging in my head about my slow progress. I felt I was not good enough. I hated making mistakes in front of the tutor. The whole experience made me anxious. The fun was gone and when I quit I felt relieved. I had successfully sabotaged myself. Being a student and making mistakes was a very uncomfortable experience. I was too impatient and self-critical. I was not willing to go through the learning process which involved making mistakes. Even though I was making good progress and was strongly encouraged by my tutor to continue, the negative voice in my head shouted much louder and it won out.

Around 2004 at a Jack Canfield (author of the *Chicken Soup for the Soul* series) seminar I witnessed just how judgemental I could be. Early into his presentation I began to feel annoyed and frustrated. I told myself that I knew everything he was talking about. Several hundred people had paid to listen to this. I felt that I should be up there speaking and not in the audience. A friend who was with me asked what was wrong. My body language was screaming frustration. Only then did I catch what was going on inside me. I had arrogantly dismissed Jack Canfield as boring and unoriginal. The fact that he was a world-renowned author and speaker I conveniently ignored. I was jealous of him and the nasty side of me came out to scoff and ridicule. This was a shock but also a wake-up call. I knew that this part of me was also dismissing my hopes and dreams the same way.

Being willing to see the truth of any situation, and not my spin on it, frees me from conflict and stress. In 2008 I attended a Vipassana retreat in England, which is a form of Buddhist meditation involving ten days of silent retreat in which you meditate for up to ten hours each day. Again my judgemental attitude was very present. My mind never seemed to shut up, constantly commenting on others around me, expressing opinions on everyone. This mental noise was intense and crazy. Not being allowed to talk for ten days helped me to relax and listen to myself. Within days the mental voices had everyone labelled. On the last day we were allowed speak again. Only then did I discover how deluded and insane my judgements and opinions of the other participants were. Every one of my perceptions was totally wrong. My cynical mind was living in its own little world, passing comment on everything and everyone without the need or desire for any proof. The madness was unmasked. This reinforced the need to listen carefully to my own thinking, not to judge and to find a way to regularly quieten this manic mind-chatter.

Being in a completely strange environment can be a perfect opportunity to see our patterns in action. This was the case when I was doing voluntary work in Mozambique in 2006. I took an immediate dislike to our two group leaders, taking everything they did and said personally. I felt judged by them and was convinced that they saw me as lazy and arrogant. I spent the first few days projecting my insecurities onto them. I related to them very differently to the rest of the group, keeping my distance as much as possible. This all changed a couple of days into the trip. I kept a daily journal on the trip. Going back over my entries one evening it became obvious that it was Me who was thinking this about myself, not them. I realised I was being judgemental. I was blaming them for me judging myself as being lazy and arrogant. I had resented their roles as leaders and justified it by projecting my stuff onto them. Realising this I was able to let go of my insecurities. My relationship with them changed completely as I relaxed and connected with them.

– 143 –

How we judge others can be a clear indication of how we judge ourselves. My tendency to criticise others close to me was a clear indicator of the inner self-criticism going on in my head. No wonder I often felt inadequate and insecure. If I was going to truly change and embrace a new and more meaningful future, I would need to be far more nurturing and supportive towards myself than was my norm and to cease listening to and believing everything this cynic was feeding me. The cynic was like a propagandist creating an inner world of suspicion, control and repression. It had held me captive through a combination of fear and negative thinking for long enough. While its purpose was to protect me, its methods were extremely harmful. Once I was aware of this cynic I had options. By listening to and observing myself, I began to witness this cynical attitude. I quickly became aware of the cynical assumptions and judgements of me and others that habitually popped into my head, and I began to reject them. I ceased being a victim and was taking back control. I was distancing myself from the internal chatter of the mind and turning my attention to my heart. I resolved to follow my intuition, and my heart, when I felt scared or vulnerable. The more I acted with courage and self-belief the stronger I became, which naturally weakened the cynic in my head. In turn this allowed me to see more of who I really was and how I typically held myself back in life.

Being aware of my inner world enabled me to change my response inside and out, creating new results in my life. Today, this aspect of me is still there, but very much weakened. I can easily spot it as it tries to spin its negative, fearful lies. When I spot it I let it go by ignoring it and following my heart instead. Now I habitually do the things which I resist, I push through my fears, focusing on feeling in the moment and acting with confidence.

## Food – the path to freedom

Food offers a great opportunity for finding and witnessing our patterns in life. Food is more than just a basic need; it offers an intimate and unique experience of ourselves for each of us. Our habits, fears, preferences, prejudices and emotional blocks are always present in our relationship with food. There is no hiding place here. How we eat, what we eat and our attitude to eating all tell us so much about ourselves. Our emotional history and psychological profile are potentially staring back up at us from our dinner plates. The patterns of lack, control and cynicism also played out in my relationship with food. My personal issues were exposed in my relationship with food. I often went on strict food plans and detoxifying programmes. This was a way of feeling in control. While I loved food, I craved my comfort foods such as breads, biscuits, chocolate, pastries, tea and coffee. I looked forward to these foods each day. They were the highlight of a day for me. I had a lot of emotional investment in food. My eating habits deteriorated at weekends when the intake of comfort food and alcohol increased.

One particular detox programme I did involved a diet free from all dairy, wheat, meat, caffeine, processed food and alcohol for twenty-eight days. During this programme I had no emotional escape through comfort food. In the past when I felt frustrated or unsettled I would use food to ease it. I was shocked by how much time I spent thinking about food over the twenty-eight days. I invested huge energy focusing on future meals and savoury treats. I thought about what I would have for lunch as I ate breakfast, and later for dinner as I ate my lunch. I was rarely in the moment as I ate. I had underestimated the extent to which food was an emotional comfort.

The experience taught me to listen to my body when deciding what and when to eat. Living in the future in my head disconnected me from the moment and therefore, from how I was feeling, missing the body's signals in relation to being full, or what to eat. As long as I continued to avoid the present my future would change very little. Change can only happen in this moment and by avoiding this moment I was robbing myself of any hope of real and lasting change.

The detox experience reminded me that my future was determined by the present-moment choices. This was reaping what I sow in action: sow now and reap later. What I ate now was either contributing to a healthy, fit future or a sick, debilitating future. So I had to start noticing when I felt full, what felt right to eat and drink in each moment, use my body to guide me in relation to food and drink. If I listened only to my head, I would be drunk most nights and seriously obese.

This relationship with food also mirrors my beliefs, fears, hopes and desires about life. The quantity and content of my dinner plate reflected my view of life. I hated waste and always cleared my plate, eating past the body's satiety signals. Eating crisps, chocolate and other comfort food was a reaction to feelings of insecurity. While my body was saying, 'I don't need this junk,' my head said the opposite.

Detoxifying the body through diet is ultimately pointless if we ignore emotional issues still held in the body. The roots of our food issues are generally emotionally based and we can never eat or starve our way through them. My hoarding of sugar-rich food and indulgence in alcohol were all about avoiding feeling the real issues in my body. Even making sure I always cleared my plate was about wanting to feel OK. Food was a comfort blanket from deeper emotional problems.

The body is highly intelligent. It knows what it needs in terms of nutrition and that is why it is so important to pay attention to the messages the body gives us throughout the day. We need to be in rapport with the body. Unresolved issues and painful memories are stored in the body until we are ready to feel them fully and release them. Dr Candace Pert in her book *Molecules of Emotion* describes the body as the unconscious mind where repressed traumas caused by overwhelming emotion are stored. Such repressed memories can be so strong as to have physical manifestations such as paralysis or impaired use of specific limbs.

When I was in therapy just prior to my marriage ending I experienced strong emotions. They surfaced as I opened up to the therapist causing my body to shake uncontrollably. Feeling these emotions, while difficult, was liberating as it was the beginning of the end of being controlled by old painful feelings of self-loathing. I was letting go of old pain in my body, which had been a powerful block in my life. Choosing to ignore the painful memories would have weakened my ability to listen to my body signals resulting in continued poor eating habits.

Food is a very clear mirror showing me what I really think and believe about myself and how I am coping with life. My relationship with food reflects my relationship with myself. If I can love and accept who I am, then the need to get drunk, eat junk food or do crash diets ends. Food can be the doorway towards a richer, more balanced and contented life. Use it as a means of raising your self-awareness, noticing the habits and routines you have around food. Notice what feelings come up as you eat or drink certain things, what are your triggers for binge eating, binge drinking, comfort eating or restricting yourself. Ask yourself if you use food as a means of feeling in control in life. Or is it something you view as purely functional, for survival? Would your eating habits change in any way if you were happy with yourself and your life?

As with all relationships in your life, there are hidden

messages about yourself in your relationship with food. Look at your relationship with food honestly and objectively. Slow down, pay attention and be curious about this aspect of your life. What you discover will amaze you.

No pattern is exclusively destructive or negative. Every pattern serves a purpose and therefore has a potential positive impact also. For example the control pattern can help keep me focused on completing a project or maintaining self-discipline in relation to a health and fitness regime. If I accept that what I resist persists, in other words by fighting something I am energising it and making it more of a problem than it really is, then resistance is an indicator of what needs to be dealt with rather than avoided. A potential positive impact of the lack mentality is that it is good for spotting what is wrong, missing and in need of attention. The lack mentality also pushed me in my career and academic pursuits. And the cynic reminds me to take nothing for granted and not let others take advantage of me, as well as being a great source of dry humour.

So every pattern contains the positive and negative, and needs to be examined with this in mind. Each pattern is an expression of who you are and you can enhance this expression of yourself more comprehensively if you are aware of the pattern and how it manifests in your daily routine. In practice, all your patterns are intertwined like a ball of wool, each one influencing and supporting the other. They operate as a single interdependent unit providing a framework or blueprint for daily living. However, such frameworks are at times very dysfunctional as illustrated in my case. At some point you need to free yourself from such patterns and develop more effective ones which improve the quality of your life.

There is no right place to begin this process, so choose any pattern to focus on. In time this creates a mindset that will enable you to spot other patterns as you progress with the work. One pattern leads to another, and another, until soon you have a rich tapestry of patterns of behaviour detailing how you actually live your life moment to moment. Since all is connected, by altering just one pattern a ripple effect will occur throughout the tapestry. Change will automatically happen in some areas of your life simply because of change in other parts of your life. This is the route to transformation. You only need to make small, incremental changes for a massive shift to happen sooner or later.

### STOP AND REFLECT

- Are the patterns of control, lack or cynicism alive in your life?

- If so, how do they impact on the quality of your life in terms of decision making, relationships, and setting and achieving your goals?

- Are you aware of the emotional relationship you have with food? What does it say about you as a person?

> - Are there negative patterns that are not mentioned here that are present in your life?
>
> - How do you hold yourself back in your relationships, career or health and fitness?
>
> - Choose a pattern to examine. List the behaviours and attitudes you are aware of for that pattern.
>
> - Then examine this list and choose those behaviours or attitudes that you could influence positively, if not stop completely. Remember, small changes in a few aspects of a pattern can bring about the complete unravelling of that pattern.
>
> - Record the process in a journal. Monitor your progress over time to gain valuable feedback and motivation.

## Beneath the patterns – the ripple effect of change

The patterns we live our lives through are largely operating outside of our awareness. The lower our self-awareness the harder it is to effect real change in our lives. Many of us will repeat the same pattern over and over in our lives, getting the same frustrating result in spite of the fact that we do not want it and desire the opposite. I call this the Elizabeth Taylor effect. From the outside looking in at the life of Elizabeth Taylor we could surmise that this was how things went for her in her relationships, getting married eight times, trying to find love, as if the solution was in a new partner.

Changing herself was the only way she could hope to achieve what she actually desired in a marriage. Only she could change her patterns and get the results she wanted in a marriage, and hoping the answer was in the perfect partner was wishful thinking. No one can solve our problems for us, they can only reflect back to us our progress or otherwise as we resolve them ourselves.

Unfortunately, instead of changing our thinking or actions, we think that by trying the same old strategies harder or even faster we will get a new result, when all we achieve is the same result faster. When we fail to change the pattern in any substantial way the end result is inevitably the same as before. No matter how fast or more intensely we act out that pattern, it can only ever deliver what it was designed to deliver, regardless of what we would have preferred.

Of course patterns are essential if we are to function in life. While most of our patterns are functional, we all have a few patterns that would be better uprooted from our psyches and replaced with more self-affirming patterns. Patterns that sabotage our dreams, goals and potential are better uprooted. Spotting these patterns is the first step and how easy this is will depend on how subtle or obvious they appear in our lives. Feedback from someone we trust and who knows us well can be very helpful when spotting our patterns. Journaling daily is a very effective tool in capturing the information that will help us to quickly spot our patterns. This develops the reflective practitioner in us, which is a powerful method of raising self-awareness.

Remember, patterns are only the pointers to the real issues in our lives. They are not the cause but the symptoms of deeper, underlying root causes, which can be accessed wherever the patterns appear in a given moment. The patterns are doorways into our subconscious, enabling us to glimpse our inner world and face the repressed emotional information. Once we can see the pattern we can then choose to address the deeper underlying issues that give life to the pattern.

The deeply held belief that "I am a mistake" was at the root of many of my patterns. These patterns served to keep me from feeling rejected, protecting me so the world would not see my mistakes. Logic had nothing to do with this. The subconscious mind is like the mind of a child, which believes everything it is told, particularly if told with emotion. The belief "I am a mistake" was buried alive inside me for all of my life. Once I discovered it I saw my life in a whole new light. Patterns appeared. As I focused on them and busted some of them, my life began to transform.

So, when you become aware of a limiting belief, the associated patterns begin to show themselves, assuming you are open to seeing them. Whichever way you approach this, spotting patterns or identifying limiting beliefs first, the easiest way to change is tracking the patterns and then busting them. Very often just spotting a pattern is sufficient to heal the underlying root cause. As with a lot of our issues in life, once it comes into full view it loses its grip on us. However, there will be occasions when trying to get rid of a pattern without addressing the root cause is just a waste of time and energy.

This is true of people who apply the concepts of positive thinking or the laws of attraction (as described in the teachings of *The Secret*) without resolving the deeper issues which have prevented them from being positive or successful in the first place. It is like putting a plaster over the wound of an amputated limb. This was true for me. No matter how often I repeated my positive affirmations, hourly and daily, telling myself "I love myself" and "my life is abundant", nothing changed. It took years for me to get this. I would not change until I identified and changed the deeper limiting belief, which was of course the polar opposite to the affirmations. And it was these limiting beliefs that were co-creating my life experiences, not the daily affirmations.

Karen's experience is another example of this. Karen came for career coaching, looking to move out of her teaching career. She claimed to be unhappy in her job and felt burnt out. Part of the coaching process can involve homework for the client, where they agree to complete specific actions in between sessions they have chosen to help them address the issues explored in the coaching sessions. Karen failed to complete the actions she had committed to in the first two sessions. So in the third session we decided to look at what was blocking her from completing the actions aimed at helping her change her career. An old emotional block quickly surfaced and the issue behind it was sexual abuse that she had experienced as a young girl. She was surprised that this had surfaced again as she believed she had dealt with it in therapy many years ago. Through coaching she realised that she had not dealt with the emotional pain from the incident completely and this was blocking her from moving forward in her life. She decided to go back for counselling and resolve it fully.

A couple of months later she returned to coaching and made rapid progress through the process. Having dealt with the deeper emotional block from the sexual abuse she had freed herself up emotionally and was able to think and see more clearly. She now realised that she loved teaching and had no desire to leave it. The real issue regarding work was bullying she was experiencing from some work colleagues. The coaching focused on her ability to tackle the bullying and build her self-esteem so that she could enjoy her work again. By the end of the coaching process she had reconnected with her passion for teaching and went on to be promoted in her work.

For Karen, the pattern that presented itself in her coaching was one of low self-esteem; she was negative in her thinking towards herself and her work; she felt inadequate and was neglecting her health through poor eating and no exercise; she was not socialising and was allowing herself to be manipulated by family members. Trying to tackle this pattern through positive thinking strategies and a career change was pointless and would have made no lasting improvement. This was because the deeper underlying root cause needed to be identified and released. Once she dealt with the root cause the associated pattern began to weaken and was easier to uproot and transform into a more positive and assertive pattern.

Karen's root cause was the emotional block resulting from a sexual abuse experience. It is important to remember that to instigate positive change focus must be on the emotional block that created the negative pattern of behaviour and thinking. Reacting to or getting lost in the story behind the emotional block is of limited value and will simply keep the person stuck if there is no letting go emotionally. As with all emotional blocks it was held in the body. Since the body is like a store house, holding onto any unresolved emotional issues from our past, it is no surprise that such issues, depending on how traumatic they were at the time, can have a serious negative influence on our day-to-day life. No amount of comfort eating or addictive behaviours, intellectualising or cynical dismissing will free us from such unresolved issues; they have to be faced and felt fully in order for us to be free of them once and for all.

This is why it is vital to be present in the body. The only other place we can be is in the head and that is of limited value most of the time. To let go and be more present in the body can be a challenge for many people. It seems safer and more acceptable to be operating in life from the head, always analysing, thinking and problem solving. I'm not saying these activities are irrelevant, they are essential for balanced living. However, we tend to rely on them too much and undervalue the body's intelligence. In practice we need to be using our head as the tool it is meant to be, subservient to the body rather than the other way around. Einstein summarised it well when he said, 'The intuitive mind is a sacred gift and the rational mind is a faithful servant. We have created a society that honours the servant and has forgotten the gift.'

Working with the body and opening your heart as part of this process is essential. If you are not able to be compassionate towards yourself, then how will you allow yourself to see the things you have up to now refused to see or own as your stuff? To be compassionate is to be accepting, open and forgiving. You are seeking to understand and help You.

In any moment when a pattern is happening, all the information required to break this pattern and heal the underlying cause is available. In other words, if you can become aware of the pattern as it is happening, you can tune into this experience and get a deeper sense and insight into what is really going on beneath the surface. I remember in the early days of my relationship with Claire, I reacted to her crying about something that I felt was insignificant. I was holding back from comforting her, feeling it was not a good idea to hug her or hold her. In that moment I became aware of my attitude. I was judging her crying as self-pity and neediness, which was making me impatient and intolerant. Once I realised what I was doing I choose to let go of this attitude. I opened up to her, held her and supported her rather than judged her. Spotting my habitual response to crying as it was happening, enabled me to change my response, change the pattern, and create a different outcome for both of us. All this happened in a split second. The impact of the different outcome reinforces the new behaviour next time.

Sometimes you miss the moment but that does not mean the opportunity is lost. The beauty of hindsight is that you can also go back to that moment and relive the experience without the emotional interference, using visualisation for example. As you revisit the moment you can unpack all the underlying information that created the pattern. In this way you get the insight needed to resolve and transform the pattern in all the areas of your life where it manifests.

Focus on one pattern at a time. Notice when and how it appears. Become familiar with the pattern so that in time you can spot it quickly. Eventually you will be so aware of it and alert to it that you will notice it appearing within you before it ever gets a chance to express itself externally through your words or actions. As you notice it appearing or as it is happening choose to do something different, or opposite to it. By counteracting the pattern you change the energy completely. In time, the pattern will weaken and fade.

There is no mystery here. Once you are aware of what is going on you can do something about it. By interrupting the pattern at a single point you are impacting on the whole pattern through the ripple effect. This is why change can be so simple – much of it often happens automatically after some initial effort by you, and once enough momentum has built up it ripples out through the full pattern causing other behaviours associated with the pattern to fall away. Change may not be easy, but it is definitely simple. We often need massive effort at the start to break through the resistance of the pattern. Sooner or later, as the pattern weakens, the effort required lessens and new behaviours that seemed impossible become part of our normal daily life.

Below is a sample of the behaviours common to each of the patterns discussed. This gives you an overview of how the three patterns showed up in my life on a daily basis. There will be other behaviours specific to your own life not listed below. Each behaviour or attitude highlights an opportunity to interrupt that pattern and change the energy and direction to create a different result. Two or more people can of course have similar patterns but the root causes are unlikely to be the same. A pattern of hoarding and comfort eating may reflect the need for security and safety, but the trigger or root of these behaviours will be unique for each person. Therefore, it is not wise to generalise or make assumptions as to why one behaves in a certain way. Spotting the pattern is useful in understanding the self, but digging deeper to the emotional root of the pattern is the only way you can know for sure what your real issue is about.

Also, the behaviours in a pattern are not necessarily unique to that pattern. They can and often do appear in more than one pattern. This is how patterns overlap and reinforce each other using the same thinking and behaviours. While you may have some of the behaviours listed below in a certain pattern, it does not necessarily mean that you have that pattern dominating you. However, the more items from the list you can recognise in your own life then the more likely it is that that particular pattern is alive in you. Whether it is a problem or not is a different question and one only you can answer.

## Pattern of lack

1. Buying two or more of certain things when one is enough.

2. Hoarding.

3. Finishing meals or clearing the plate, beyond the point of feeling full.

4. Seeing a half full glass of liquid as half empty.

5. Collecting excess information when undertaking a task or project.

6. Excessively editing material to the point of incomprehension.

7. Being tight or mean with money (or other items).

8. When organising a public event, worrying not enough people will turn up.

9. Gathering items such as paper, pens, sweets left after meetings for your own personal use.

10. Wearing clothes to the point of shabbiness, when you have plenty of new choices in the wardrobe.

11. Rarely wearing your favourite items of clothing for fear of wearing them out too soon.

12. Reuse unwashed dishes to eat from (within the same day).

13. Eat left over food cooked a day or two before, even though it's nutritionally void.

14. Decide not to do things because they are too expensive.

15. Feeling there is not enough time to get all you want done in a day.

16. Often feel you are not good enough.

17. Focus habitually on what is missing, absent or wrong.

18. Regularly drive the car on an almost empty tank of fuel.

19. Some areas of your life are very cluttered.

20. You have a deep dislike for waste of any type.

## Pattern of control

1. Staying in the head, avoiding physical things and activities.

2. Avoiding situations which cause you to feel uncomfortable.

3. Not communicating.

4. Holding back information from others who need to receive it.

5.  Excessive scheduling and planning.

6.  Doing all the driving and/or reacting aggressively or impatiently towards other drivers on the road.

7.  Rigid routines for meals, activities etc.

8.  Extremes of any kind (it is the other side of control; it is the same energy).

9.  Labelling, judging and criticising others so that you don't have to change or try new things.

10. Emotionally neutral; repressing, denying, rationalising or intellectualising your emotions.

11. Not taking risks.

12. Not being spontaneous.

13. Not delegating.

14. Hoarding.

15. People pleasing and trying to avoid conflict.

16. Anticipating future outcomes, second guessing peoples' responses in conversations.

17. Trying to get others to change, highlighting their faults and failings.

18. Judging others who control.

19. Reacting strongly to being controlled or manipulated.

20. Bullying or being bullied

## Pattern of cynicism

1. Distrustful of self and/or others.

2. Sneering and sarcastic.

3. Dismissive attitude; reject others and their ideas.

4. Pessimistic and negative in outlook.

5. Usually assume the worst.

6. Risk averse

7. Arrogant, condescending.

8. Defensive and over-sensitive.

9. Judgemental attitude.

10. Poor listener; poor communicator.

11. Give up easily or quickly.

12. Feel safe and comfortable with the familiar.

13. Worrier.

14. Habitually focus on past/future negatively.

15. Resentful, jealous, hold grudges.

16. Quick to condemn.

17. Moan, complain, gossip a lot.

18. Rationalise and trivialise emotions.

19. Nasty, hurtful, critical.

20. Manipulate and /or take advantage of others.

## STOP AND REFLECT

✎ Can you recognise similar patterns in your life?

✎ What one pattern in your life would you most like to change?

✎ What pattern would you most like to adopt?

✎ Are you aware of any unfinished business (emotionally speaking) from your past that you need to acknowledge and resolve?

✎ Are you comfortable in and with your body? If yes, how do you know?

✎ If no, what are you prepared to do to change this and create a loving relationship with your body?

✎ Keep a journal for one month and record where and when specific behaviours and attitudes show up each day. You will see patterns arising over the month if you record the information accurately, i.e. consistently and honestly.

✎ Get feedback from trusted friends on what they see in you in terms of your patterns or habits of interacting, decision making, taking risks, expressing your feelings, being assertive, making friends, supporting others, looking after yourself and anything else you consider relevant to your situation.

✎ Notice your environment – your home, your car, your job, your clothes, your bank balance, your friends, your family, your hobbies, your social scene – everything is feedback about you in terms of your beliefs, attitude and patterns of behaviour and thinking. Examine this feedback objectively for more insights into yourself. All this information is right in front of you, open up to what it has to tell you about you. Positive change starts from here.

From the above lists you have the opportunity to see how a pattern, once it has been pinpointed, can be deconstructed in a step-by-step fashion. Each item listed is an example of that pattern in action and addressing some of the items weakens the pattern. You can start where it is easiest, tackling those aspects or behaviours which require the least time and effort from you. Such a baby-step approach slowly builds your confidence as you see your progress evolving and eventually you find yourself tackling the more substantial aspects of the pattern with less drama than you originally feared.

This process is deceptively simple but do not underestimate the challenge involved. The process is not always easy, at least not initially. Resilience and a strong desire for inner change are essential ingredients for optimum results. This process of pattern spotting and busting will free you from your past. It is a method that will work for anyone.

## Heart whispers – lessons in living

Stumbling through life, trying to find enlightenment while being exceedingly cynical, I still managed to learn a lot from my experiences and benefit from them. This shows that anyone can do the same. To spot your strengths and weaknesses, your fears, insecurities and deepest desires is a no-brainer. Notice more as you live each day, reflect more and be open to the learning process that is life. It may be challenging, requiring courage and determination but this visceral trip, which only ends when you die, is a one-way ticket to self-acceptance. I highly recommend it as the lessons you will learn about you will equally amaze and renew you.

Overall the most important lesson I have learned so far is to follow my heart. This is such an obvious one that you might call it a cliché and you would be right. It is a cliché because it is true. Clichés are those things in life we have become numbed to, take for granted and easily dismiss. We have forgotten that every cliché started life as a truth or piece of wisdom.

Living from the heart is the most fundamental lesson there is. All else springs from it and serves to reinforce it. While it may seem simple, beginning to live from the heart was incredibly challenging for me. My head-centred living was anything but heart focused. Leaving the head to be present in the body was my way of moving from the head to the heart. Unravelling the patterns that had kept me head-bound were part of this process or journey.

The lessons learned in this process remind me of the importance of living from the heart and keep me on this journey, deepening the work and the connection with myself. The head will shout all the time at me about what I should be doing and why I was stupid to say that or do this. The heart never shouts, it only whispers to me and I need to be quiet, calm and still to hear it. It is my greatest resource and most powerful teacher. If I follow its lead I will always be fine.

## Learning to follow my heart

Change is constant and trying to control or resist it

is stupid. I can influence how I change in terms of my attitude, my habits and the quality of my life, by enhancing my self-awareness. Holding on to the past serves no positive purpose, it acts as a block. I had to choose to stop hiding behind blame and excuses for not changing. I needed to take ownership of my reactions, thoughts and feelings. Personal responsibility expanded the choices available to me in responding to life in each moment.

Whatever I was looking for, be it happiness, peace, success or recognition, only I could allow it into my life. I had to stop searching for someone else to do it for me. Focusing on understanding the self-help theories was pointless if they were not applied. I needed to be honest with myself and be open to life's feedback. Only the truth sets anyone free and speaking my truth sets me free from my fears.

In the past I had dismissed the power of incremental change. But taking small steps to create the change I desired turned out to be the only way forward. Observing myself in a neutral manner was part of this work. I began to witness my judgements and assumptions. My inner critic stood out and became easier to address. Becoming aware of my internal cynic enabled me to step back from it and not identify with it. I stopped taking things personally, which was a huge relief. It was not easy, persistence and patience were required. When I was struggling I thought of the words of Michaelangelo: "Ancora Imparo" (I am still learning).

Constantly learning from life requires humility, while

at the same time embracing my potential and talents. I had to acknowledge the success I had achieved. In other peoples' eyes I was successful but I had been blind to it. Gradually I accepted my achievements and strengths which enabled me to embrace new challenges and significant change in all areas of my life.

Part of this transforming process was to be present in my body, rather than living in the head – do more physical things, feel and sense more, think with my whole body. Rejection of my body was a very effective way of staying out of it. I always felt unattractive and so my body was never a comfortable place to be. Feeling fat equalled rejection. This would not change while I was rooted in my head. I was a "head case", not trusting or believing in myself as a person. It was easier to live life through someone else. For example I read self-help books with another person, usually a girlfriend, as my point of reference. I focused on her issues, as I perceived them, and how the self-help material could help her. I ignored my own perspective. I needed to accept that I had no control over other people or events. By taking ownership of what I was responsible for, my response to life each day, my life became less stressful and more productive.

The only way to resolve my personal issues was to come back to me, to live in my body fully and work with both my head and heart. Both were essential for a balanced existence. The years of self-development had helped me realise this. Even though I had failed to find enlightenment or the route to bliss, the seeking had helped me to finally understand on a gut level that I had all I needed. What I sought was inside me all along; trusting and accepting was all I ever needed to do.

This helped me to change in so many ways. One way was in how I approached goal setting, both in terms of what I set goals for and how I achieved them. Any goal setting I did was mainly focused on my career. Through my work as a coach and trainer I was familiar with the range of goal setting strategies and processes from people like Brian Tracy, Napoleon Hill, Jack Canfield and others. I had used vision boards, goal cards, affirmations, visual aids and other goal setting strategies. Some worked better than others, and all were reliant on my willingness to remain focused, positive and resilient.

Occasionally I applied these strategies for material items. When a friend of mine bought a luxury car it awakened in me a desire for the same thing and a sense that I could actually afford one. I set myself a goal to own a similar car, a BMW. This was a challenging goal for me at that time, since my driving life up to then was in middle of the range cars such as Opels and Nissans. I identified exactly what I wanted in the car – the year, the colour, the model, mileage range, and the price range. I set the price at a level which on the face of it seemed a bit unrealistic, i.e. cheap. I got two photographs of the exact car I wanted, placed one on my bedroom mirror and the other on the centre of the steering wheel of my Nissan. Thus, the image of this car was constantly in my face. Over the period of three months I visited a number of luxury car dealerships and surfed the net for deals. Repeatedly I was told I would not get the car I wanted for that price. But I persisted and kept looking. I found my car, it was the right colour and model, the mileage was slightly over my upper limit and the price was bang on what I wanted.

This reminded me never to underestimate the power of focus. When I get complete clarity on what I want, then the only thing that stands between me and my clear goal is my passion to reach it. One day I decided to write down in detail what I wanted in my ideal partner. I did this after my break-up with Triona, realising that I needed to get clear about what I valued in a partner and not simply chase after any single female who looked good. I needed direction and clarity. Two months later Claire walked into my life. She ticked all of the boxes apart from age and height. In spite of my initial misgivings I soon realised that these two factors were the least important.

The cynic in me used to dismiss goal setting as just a gimmick and too much effort to even bother with. In truth, goal setting is an attitude and is essential for anyone who wants to be effective in life. This can range from planning a holiday, organising a party, starting a new job or course, to starting a family, buying a house, creating a new lifestyle or career, deepening a relationship or raising self-awareness. While my approach to goal setting had been ad-hoc and inconsistent, there were some elements common to my goal setting experiences. These were a strong desire for the goal, total clarity on what I wanted, a strong inner belief in my ability to achieve it and a persistent focus on working towards the goal regardless of setbacks.

All my attempts to set and achieve financial goals succeeded only partially, and in some instances failed completely. The reason for this was my own lack of self-belief in relation to achieving the goal. This demonstrated how important it was to feel that this goal was right for me and that I truly believed it would happen. Since the process of achieving any goal required that I be part of that process, it was vital for me to engage in it with ease and confidence. Too often I created blockages and resistance to realising my goals through impatience, desperation or lack of trust.

Trust is central in this whole process. I had to be willing to both trust myself and the process of goal setting. It is not blind trust, it is a trust based on self awareness and self acceptance. It is grounded in the physicality of my being, my abilities and resources. It requires a compassionate approach allowing myself to take risks, learn from my mistakes and keep myself motivated during the difficult moments.

I set a goal of reaching and maintaining a weight of eleven stone through regular exercise and healthy eating. I was not interested in any strict dieting or cutting out all my favourite foods. I wanted to balance my lifestyle more so that I could enjoy foods such as chocolate, ice cream and cakes, wine and beer while still feeling fit and healthy. When I reached my target weight it was easier to stay at that weight because I had not made radical or extreme dietary changes. It was a lifestyle change with regular exercise at least three days per week. This initially took massive focus, determination and persistence as I had to overcome the resistance I felt to changing old habits of comfort eating and TV watching. As part of this process I paid close attention to how I was feeling watching TV and not comfort eating. I refused to comfort eat and instead simply focused on what my body was feeling in those moments and in this way, gradually the comfort eating desire fell away. This made it easier to keep exercising. Both aspects of this process fed and reinforced each other enabling me to realise the goal in a matter of months.

Today the only goals I set are the ones that feel right. In my heart I know they are right. I use vision boards and journaling to keep me focused on the goal without obsessing about it. Once I have the clarity for the goal, I work out what I can do next to achieve it. And then I do it. Depending on the goal I may use some form of feedback mechanism to monitor my progress and keep me motivated. Overall this process is simple, relaxed and fluid.

## Learning to follow my heart at work

For the past fifteen years or more I have spent most of my work repeating the same message to all I met: do what you love in life and life will take care of you. What fascinated me about the people I worked with as a coach was that they knew what they would love to do in life. Knowing it was never the problem; it may have appeared to be at the start, but after some questioning and probing their dreams or ambitions came back to them. The problem was their own fears of pursuing them. People were always scared of going for what was in their hearts. Not just about careers and new work – this was also true for relationships.

I had let my own fears drive me from teaching, a career I was skilled at and had potential to excel at. As a guidance counsellor in the secondary school system some of my teaching colleagues considered me to be management material, and on a few occasions I was encouraged to apply for specific managerial positions in local schools as they came up. I could not see this in myself and, while flattered by it all, was good at dismissing it. The only person holding me back in my career was me.

As I progressed in the world of work and became my own boss, the challenges grew more intense and personal. The lessons learned reflected the deeper nature of these challenges. I recall a period when I was unable or unwilling to teach certain topics such as values and beliefs or rapport on our coaching course because these were areas or skills in my life which I had yet to grasp and integrate. I resisted teaching them as I had not embodied them in my life – all I had was an intellectual understanding of them. It is said that you teach best what you need to know most. What I was always excellent at teaching and talking about was the need to do what you love in life, to follow your heart and be yourself. While these were big picture statements, I was very slow to tease out the detail of them. For example, being aware of your values in life is essential in finding the work at which you would shine. I took a long time to do this for myself.

The lessons I was teaching others were relevant to me. For a time I had the arrogance to think I was applying what I was teaching, that I was further along the road of personal effectiveness than many others. My ability to fool myself was remarkable. Only when I began to pay attention to my words, actions and thoughts did I realise how much I was fooling myself. All the times I had been passionately exhorting others to follow their heart and do what they love in life, I was really talking to myself. I was trying to get me to wake up, get up and get working at what I really wanted.

Like those who came to me for career guidance and coaching I needed an independent observer to help me see what I was doing to limit myself. Through them I learned the importance of opening my heart to the world of work and letting it tell me what to do. I have no doubt that everyone can work at something they enjoy if they make it their aim. There is nothing unrealistic about it. What is required is the commitment to achieve it and willingness to accept the consequences of achieving it.

While much of my focus had been on work and career, relationships of all kinds formed a significant part of this. The major breakthroughs in my life came about through the relationships I had, including the painful ones. The close relationships I forged as my career developed provided the impetus and space for some profound personal healing and altered the course of my life completely.

## Learning to follow my heart in relationships

Relationships are the most powerful arena for learning about ourselves. Other people act as mirrors for us, reflecting back to us aspects of ourselves that need to be acknowledged and integrated. Blaming others for our problems only serves to keep us locked in the victim mentality, powerless and frustrated.

Relationships are the one place in life where we cannot hide from ourselves indefinitely. When we are being honest we learn the truth of who we are through our relationships. Often, in the early days of my marriage, I would ask Laura what she saw in me, why she chose to be with me? I found it hard to accept that a girl as attractive as her would be interested in someone like me. I simply felt unworthy. This same feeling came up again in my relationship with Triona.

These relationships highlighted my self-rejection. After the marriage break-up my mother reminded me of the time I asked her, a few days before the wedding, if she had any doubts when she was getting married. She replied that if I was having any doubts I should delay the wedding until I was sure it was the right thing to do. I told her that it was OK; I was looking forward to the wedding day itself and felt it would be a great day for everyone. So even back then I was aware that this was not the right thing to do and yet I chose to ignore my intuition. I was rejecting me, ignoring my intuition and focusing on other peoples' expectations.

Fear of getting hurt, betrayed, abused, abandoned are just some of the reasons why we hold back in relationships of all kinds. We prefer to manage or even manipulate the relationship to feel safe and secure. Such behaviours bring about the very thing we are trying to avoid. Choosing to trust ourselves allows others to be themselves in the relationship. By trusting ourselves we refer to our own intuition or gut feelings more, we are aware of how we feel and act accordingly. We have more self-control and are less inclined to exert control over others. Choosing to trust that we will be fine whatever happens, that we can cope, enables us to be more open, present and, therefore, authentic. When we are authentic our relationships shine and blossom.

The most fundamental and deepest relationships we have in our lives, for many of us, are with our families; the ones we grow up in and the ones we create. The experiences of growing up in my adopted family, finding and bonding with my birth family, leaving my wife and her family and then becoming a father and creating a whole new family life with Claire and Josh, all deeply influenced and moulded me into the man I am today. Our families are our clearest and strongest mirrors in life, providing the potential for greater self-acceptance.

Finding my birth mother was significant in enhancing my sense of self. The journey of separation, living apart for years and reconnecting as adults with my birth family was intense. The emotions and insecurities associated with the experience were challenging. Growing up I had to fill in the gaps in myself, I had to fake feeling normal.

All the time I was aware of chunks of information missing inside me and didn't know how to handle it. This fed my drive to seek out cures, solutions, comfort and relief.

Fortunately I grew up in a healthy family environment. My adoptive parents taught me much simply by doing their best as parents. If I could meet my dad again I would hug him and thank him for his guidance. He instilled in me a high regard for education and intellect, for honesty and integrity. Through his actions I learned how important it is to be true to myself. He told me life was tough and that family mattered most. After he died people would say to me, 'If you get to be half the man your father was, you'll be doing just fine.' I could not agree more.

The arrival of the birth family into my life was a catalyst for change. Initially they were a source of comfort. When I was with them I felt like partying. Their ease at giving hugs every time we met was, at first, uncomfortable but over time I began to enjoy it. They taught me to hug and to express my emotions. I began to open up. They brought more fun into my life, showing me a side of myself that had been too often hidden away. Their presence helped me to open my heart.

Slowly I became aware of my resistance to being present even with them, no doubt a result of the challenge of being more in my heart. They became a powerful mirror for my deeper issues, triggering my stuff in a variety of ways. That familiar sense of unease was still there and was more obvious in their company. My need to impress them and be accepted was deepening this awareness. Through them I saw, again, how I feared rejection and kept people at a distance.

Both of my families in their own ways have challenged me to take my place as a man, a son, a brother and a father. Accepting these invitations consciously has helped to transform me from the shy, insecure teenager to the assured, open and present man.

The more present I am in any relationship the healthier it is. A closed heart only serves to close down communication and any hope of a real relationship. By trusting my heart and letting it guide me in my interactions with others I am honouring both of us. This is being authentic and it builds trust.

All this is a work in progress and is dependent upon the quality of the relationship I have with myself. The extent to which I trust and appreciate myself powerfully impacts the nature and quality of my relationships with others. Embracing both of my families as part of who I am, as well as appreciating my physicality, expressing my creativity and acting from my heart have proven to be essential elements in deepening my self-acceptance, enabling me to be my own man.

## It is all about self-acceptance

I have spent much of my life in a sort of suspended animation, just waiting for it to begin. In the back of my mind I held the belief that my life had not yet started. I had this sense of persistent impatience for things to change and get better, for my life to transform into what I thought it should be, and then, I believed, I would be living properly. A typical attitude I had was: "I will be happy when …". There was always a reason to delay feeling content or happy now. Something was always missing or incomplete.

There were many moments of happiness and joy but lurking beneath the surface was a disquiet and discontentedness. Drink, cigarettes, chocolate, travel and sex couldn't keep it away for very long. All the therapists, counsellors, healers and teachers I worked with failed to shift it. Of course shifting it was down to me, only I could ever be responsible for me and blaming others for not fixing me was bullshit. Then one day something simple happened. It occurred to me that this underlying feeling was just that, a feeling, and so I could choose to stop taking it so seriously if I wanted. From that day on I changed my relationship with this feeling, I no longer tried to ignore or manage it. I accepted its presence and allowed myself to feel it. I took back my power by choosing to respond to this feeling in a different way. That is what made the difference.

This strategy of letting go, of not reacting to the feeling, but allowing myself to feel it, was one I began to practise regularly. I became calmer and more peaceful. Worries and fears were not taking a grip of me as they had in the past. I was responding to them differently, as soon as I became aware of them I acknowledged and felt them. I was present more often. Being more self-confident enabled me to stay in the present. All issues and problems were much easier to deal with if I stayed in the present and faced them as they were.

The degree to which I have mastered this self-acceptance can be measured by the extent to which I am ready and willing to stay open to uncomfortable information in each moment. In 2009 I gave a talk to a group on living life from your heart and the feedback received was positive from all but one. This person's feedback was verging on nasty. My initial reaction was shock, anger and disappointment. I wanted to tell her what I thought of her feedback and why she was wrong. I wanted her to see that she was projecting her stuff onto me. Then I challenged myself to re-read the feedback without reacting to it and see if any of what was said might be true. As I did I was able to hear what was being said in the feedback, I got an understanding of where she was coming from and I realised parts of it were accurate.

By staying present and open I was able to accept this experience for what it was, one person's experience of a talk I gave. In the past I would have reacted by focusing on the negative and retreating into the head, which only deepening my resentment. Having to be on the defensive all the time was demanding. Sooner or later something would have to give. Eventually I reached a point where I felt I had suffered enough and was now willing to change my attitude. Letting go of pain and guilt is a moment-by-moment task – over time it becomes easier and eventually, the feelings are just a memory. Never underestimate the importance and power of staying present and dealing with what is actually in the present moment.

The degree to which I had been rejecting Me and my legitimate experiences for so long was shocking. I realised that for any healing to happen it was vital that I accept all of my experiences. I needed to accept the fact I had such hatred and dislike of myself, that I rejected myself so thoroughly, that I saw myself as a mistake and was not worthy of anything in life, that I deserved nothing and no one. I needed to accept this as part of me and my legacy. Once I did this only then could I actually learn from it all.

Doing this was a first step. By accepting myself without demanding changes or adjustments I was allowing myself to be present, to be open and trusting. By embracing all I had been resisting and going through the block (the sum of all my fears) I was turning my misery into my power.

Rachel Keogh in her book *Dying to Survive* details her life as a drug addict from the age of eleven and the many failed attempts to quit. She finally succeeded in kicking her drug addiction in her late twenties. This happened after she decided to stop trying to quit and actually accepted her drug addiction. She chose to stop fighting or resisting it. By embracing her addiction she was going with the flow. She trusted the process and took the necessary steps for transformation. These steps lay waiting for her as soon as she stopped trying to force change. Only when she let go and relaxed into the very life she was resisting could she finally begin to see a real way forward. Surrendering control is a prerequisite for transformation in life.

Part of the process of self-acceptance is acknowledging when I have not accepted me and my past experiences. This is easily seen in old relationships. In rejecting others I am in that moment rejecting some aspect of myself. This does not mean I need to accept everyone and be their friend. What it does mean is that I see each individual as an opportunity for understanding myself by being present to them in a non-judgemental way, listening to them and genuinely striving to understand their position by allowing them to be themselves rather than wanting them to change to suit me in some way.

When I reject another person, in any encounter, immediately an opportunity arises to learn about my patterns of thinking and behaviour that held me back or caused me to reject (both that person and myself). These people act as mirrors for me and provide me with golden opportunities to discover the truth about me rather than continuing to blame them and the world around me.

When I rejected myself in any way I became powerless. I became a victim. This happened when I did not accept who I was, when I was not content with myself, when I craved change in so many ways, when I was restless, dissatisfied, frustrated, impatient, always wanted more, insatiable, was afraid to develop my skills and talents, deliberately limited myself and held myself back from full engagement with life in different ways.

I was not present to me because I did not like or want to be that person with all the so called horrible feelings and emotions and pain. So I kept a distance from Eoin, I refused to own him. Living in the head meant I could avoid myself and observe rather than be myself. I was in a state of disassociation, one step removed from experiencing, not participating, just observing and commenting. To be present was scary, unpredictable, uncomfortable and uncontrollable.

While this is a journey available to us all, each journey is unique and incomparable to any other. Thus my journey can only be experienced by me. I have to take the steps on this journey alone, turning inwards, walking back to me, towards my heart and home, accepting who I am. It has an ending only in death, and until then we are constantly learning and growing ... or resisting it!

Every day provides me with evidence of my self-acceptance. The fact that I am in a relationship where I feel loved for who I am, and where I love my partner and my son for who they are, tells me how far I have come. I know now that I am both the hero and victim in my own life story. Every day I get to choose which one I want to be, and needless to say it is much more fun and more rewarding being my own hero rather than hoping and waiting for one to turn up and save me.

So ...

This journey of self-acceptance is exciting and hard,

but it is the best one available. To turn back or stop at any point would be madness. Trust is a huge part of all of this. Trust in myself that what I am doing is the right thing for me, that I know what I want and who I am. Strengthening this trust requires that I listen more deeply to myself and others, I take more risks, follow my heart, let go more and have fun. In this way, self-growth becomes a life choice and a powerful way of being.

Your personal lessons are waiting to be learned and can only be done by deepening your self awareness. As part of this there are certain things you can incorporate into your life that will inevitably replace the limiting and sabotaging patterns. These attitudes and behaviours are available to all and will benefit those who adopt them. They are presented in Section Three as universal life lessons. By practising these lessons or principles you are guaranteed to raise your level of awareness and transform your life.

## STOP AND REFLECT

🖐 What personal lessons have you learned from your life experience to date?

🖐 Are you living your life lessons?

Some questions that can help to uncover personal life lessons:

🖐 What has worked in your life and what has it taught you?

🖐 What has not worked in your life and what has it taught you?

🖐 If you could start your life over again knowing what you know now, what (if any) changes would you make?

✽ If you could go back in time to when you were thirteen years old (or an alternative age when you were more innocent and hopeful about life) and give yourself some advice, what would you say to that young person?

✽ What are the defining moments in your life? Such moments are rich with learning. Identify as many lessons as you can from these key moments.

And ...

✽ Are you good at living from your heart? If not, what stops you?

✽ How can you bring your heart more into your everyday life?

# **Section** THREE

## Life Lessons
## From Head to Heart:
### The Shortcut Home

## LEARNING THE LESSONS WITHOUT THE DRAMA

The following six life lessons or life principles incorporate the learning gained from my experiences and from the self-development work I have done both on myself and with others. The lessons are generic, relevant to all of us regardless of our stage of life or level of awareness. Initially, they may seem obvious, simple and, consequently, easy to take for granted. Too often we can dismiss such information as being simplistic, trite or beneath us. The fact is if we apply these lessons in earnest in our daily lives, we will transform our lives and ourselves with it. We will be less inclined to focus on the drama of our daily experiences and see things from a more constructive, clearer and empowering perspective.

Each life lesson contains both the process of how to achieve it and the outcome of achieving it. Thus the instructions for use are wrapped up in the description of each lesson. While the lessons are simple, this does not mean they are always easy to apply. They require determination, persistence and patient practise.

The multitude of benefits that accrue from living these lessons begin to show up in your life very quickly. As all the lessons are interconnected you can begin with any one of them and allow yourself to be drawn into the practice of the others as you focus on one or two. Focusing on one enhances and supports the practice of the others.

Devise your own strategy for incorporating them into your daily life. Know that as you do you will change and transform how you live in many subtle and sometimes very obvious ways. There is no timeline associated with the lessons and no deadline for achieving them. The whole process is simply a moment-to-moment experience. Your own awareness is central to all of this. It is the fundamental ingredient in the successful application of the lessons. And their application will enhance your awareness, which in turn will reinforce your commitment to the lessons and the benefits you will gain.

## Lesson One: be present

*'Wherever you are, be there!'*
This lesson involves slowing down, observing myself and life more closely and more often, accepting this moment now as it is.

## Slow down

Doing more things and doing them faster was my aim in life. To achieve more by managing my time better and using systems to make me more efficient, I used diaries, wall charts, filofaxes and goal planning sheets. My efficiency increased at the expense of my effectiveness. The key to being truly effective is to slow down enough to become aware of what I am doing. As I slow down things fall into view that previously I was unaware of. This provides more insights into me and my life. I discover so much more when I slow down. I get more of what really matters done, and done well.

In spite of my head telling me that faster is better and more desirable, little in life benefits from speed. My body suffers when I eat or drink fast, when I don't pace myself physically. When I choose to eat and drink more slowly I really taste the food, and it gives my body time to register the food intake. I recognise when I am full. In many longevity studies, one of the common traits amongst those surveyed is that they savour the act of consuming food and drink. Overindulgence is far less likely to happen when I eat and drink in this way. The body always knows when it has had enough. To slow down I need to be in the body more. I focus on my breathing to take me out of my head and into my body; this is the quickest and most effective way to slow down.

## Breathe deeply and slowly

Deep, slow breathing helps me to feel calm, to be

more focused and clearer in my thinking. It enables me to be more decisive, more peaceful and accepting of things as they are now, more aware of myself, much more present and therefore in my power. As adults we have forgotten how to breathe properly. Babies simply breathe naturally. A baby's breathing is deep and full-bodied. The stomach rises with every in-breath. It is diaphragm breathing. A deep, deliberate in-breath will bring me back into the moment by taking me out of my head and into my body. Here I have access to my power, my intuition, my awareness and my heart. The only time I can feel good is in the present.

## Feel my emotions and express them

An emotion is a means of communication for the body. It is simply energy in motion. It is important to pay attention to it and not run from it, deny it or react to it. Fear of an emotion such as anger, rage, sadness, is often caused by thinking I may lose control or be seen as unstable or weak by others. However, all I need to do is handle them responsibly. To do this I become aware of the emotion, bringing my full attention to it and breathing into it. I don't think about it or analyse it, I simply feel it and I usually notice a message, a picture, an idea or word inside me as I feel the feeling; every emotion has something to deliver. Then, once the strength of the emotion has dissipated, I can communicate the relevant information from the feeling. The key here is not to react to or from the emotion. Reacting is not being responsible for my emotions. Get the message, let the emotion go by feeling it fully and choose how to act after that.

## Accept what is now

To accept what simply is at this moment involves surrendering, letting go of ego demands – the need to control, to be right, to win, to feel different, to manipulate or challenge, to force or reject. Since I do not and cannot know the full picture in any moment, to reject or resist things as they are right now is both pointless and childish. Once I accept fully the moment as it is, I release any resistance to it and free up all my energy for positive change and development. Thus, I can accept the present, because it is the present (even though I may not like or agree with it), and I can still create a desirable future through my focused actions. My actions are focused because I have ample energy to act since I am not using it up resisting the reality of this moment. I accept this moment by breathing deeply into my body (into the moment) and becoming present. Only when I am present can I accept this moment. The irony is if I don't accept things in the moment then I am actually stuck with them for much longer than I would otherwise have been. Acceptance is the first step in making any change.

## Lesson two: lighten up

*'The only thing in life worthy of being taken seriously is the daily act of taking nothing seriously'*

This lesson asks me to be childlike (not childish), more curious (not nosy), to be fun loving, to laugh more, seek more joy, stay innocent (not ignorant) and open. And not to take myself so seriously.

### Laugh every day

When I laugh, I lighten up. This helps the body to de-stress and relax. Laughter aids healing. Norman Cousins MD in *Anatomy of an Illness* gives an excellent account of his own healing journey with cancer, citing the use of laughter as a key ingredient in his daily dose of "medicine". A good belly laugh is therapeutic. It heals me in the moment. I feel so much better after having a good gut-wrenching laugh. I choose to stop being so serious and instead I want to find and create opportunities for laughing.

## Seek joy and fun daily

When I decide to look for joy and fun in any situation, I find them. The opportunity for joy is around me always and by prioritising my desire for joy in a given situation I am ensuring that life remains predominantly lighter, more hopeful and fun. This does not preclude the need to be practical and tend to the relevant tasks in daily life. It allows me to bring a different emphasis to how I am being and how I do things. I choose to be less serious and more relaxed about things. Not taking things personally helps me to achieve and maintain this approach to my life.

## Be curious

Life is far more interesting and fun if I keep my curiosity alive. I don't mean being nosy – curiosity is about being interested, innocent, eager to learn and understand. Remaining curious for the rest of my life will help me stay young at heart and fresh in mind. It keeps my creativity alive and alert, it helps me to be a fascinating and enjoyable person to be around, and it allows me to take nothing for granted. I ask questions like I did as a child and I never accept the obvious or the bland as an answer. I realise that the more I think I know about life the more deluded I am being. Curiosity is not about intellect or intelligence; it is about imagination and inspiration. Simply explore for its own sake, learn because I can, ask questions to stay alert and see life through fresh eyes. There is no such thing as a dumb question.

## Being defenceless is the best defence

The only way to resolve conflict in my life is to stop defending myself and my opinion. Stop needing to prove myself right or better. It takes two willing parties for a fight to break out, verbal or otherwise. In my act of being defenceless I disarm the other person. With practise and persistence I begin to feel more at ease and relaxed in myself. I feel no need to justify, defend, or argue anymore. Situations sort themselves out more easily, or simply fade away. I have stopped focusing on conflict and variations of it. I focus instead on peace and stop taking things personally. It is not about being weak or a doormat. It is not about playing childish head games. It is about seeing past the fear and hurt, and seeking to communicate at a deeper level with the other person so that real connection and change can happen.

### STOP AND REFLECT

↳ Where and when do you find it easy to lighten up?

↳ What distracts you from being lighter?

↳ What would be different in your life and in you if you lived this lesson every day?

## Lesson three: focus on what matters

*'There is only one great adventure and that is inwards towards the self'*

Henry Miller

This lesson asks me to trust myself, listen to my body (intuition) and look within for the strength and confidence I seek externally. External focus is a distraction. I already have what I need. I already am what I'm looking for. I work from the inside out and celebrate my uniqueness.

### Recognise my own uniqueness

The habit of comparing myself to others feels so normal and easy to do. Yet the only outcome it brings is to feel insecure and small. I habitually put people on pedestals, people I admired and respected. And I envied their success and achievements. I would look at them or read about them and think if only I could do that or be like that. This was not done consciously. Once I became aware I was doing it, I turned it around and stopped the habit. I had to remind myself that I have talents and skills that I can express in a way that is unique to me. When I genuinely feel good enough about myself I put no one on a pedestal for anything. I see all as being on the same level doing their own thing as best they can. So I "pedestalise" no one, including myself.

I am the same as everyone else on the planet in that I am completely unique in how I do me – there is only one of me, so it is my duty to shine and let others see the real me.

## Celebrate my own achievements and contributions

Recognising my achievements requires honesty and humility. I am never standing still; I am either improving or disimproving. In some areas of my life I am improving. By acknowledging and celebrating these areas in which I am improving I reinforce them. This brings focus and I get more of what I focus on. Nothing builds confidence quicker then seeing myself make progress. I choose to see my qualities and achievements for what they are – evidence of my ability and potential.

## Choosing my attitude

I can only focus on one thought at a time. My response to my thoughts is, with practise and awareness, within my control. I observe myself regularly, listening to or watching my thoughts without judging them. This is how I raise my awareness in the moment and how I stay connected to my power.

My attitude to a person or event determines how I experience it. The attitude I bring to a conversation or to a meeting will colour how I experience it and often the end result will have been decided before I even engage with them because of my initial attitude. Focusing on what people are thinking about me is another way of avoiding Me. By focusing in this way on things and people outside of me I am blaming, avoiding, being a victim and keeping myself stuck in a space of weakness. I stop being personally responsible. The only place I need to be in any moment is present in myself. I notice when my attention drifts and bring it back to where it belongs, minding its own business, literally taking care of its own business – Me. It is imperative that I master my attitude as much as possible and be able to respond appropriately to any event rather than react to it. I am the one who determines how I think and feel, not other people and events outside of me.

## Trust my intuition

My intuition, my gut feeling, is higher intelligence, the big picture, the essence and heart of what and who I am. It is a knowing, a feeling and sense, an insight which has always been there and always will. I cannot take from it, control it or change it. It simply is part of me. Fear, doubt, analysis and judgement all shut down intuition. Following intuition is not always easy. But trusting and acting on intuition strengthens me, even though it does not mean that things will always work out the way I think I want them to. It means I am always moving in the right direction. I act on my intuition with confidence, thus making it a stronger experience and easier to relate to and act from my intuition.

## Lesson four: go with life's flow

'Water is purified by flowing, the human being by going forward'

Hindu proverb

'Be careful what you set your heart upon, for you will surely have it'

R.W. Emerson

This lesson asks me to let go regularly, choose freedom and peace, forgive and stop trying to control. Instead I can follow my heart, do what I love, identify and pursue my passions and speak my truth. Don't wait for change to happen. Act now in some way and take calculated risks.

## Let go in each moment

There are many ways I can let go and the most common approach is to forgive. This is a choice available to me always. Forgiveness is all about the self. I forgive to free myself. Every moment offers the opportunity to see things differently, to choose to let go of the issue or attitude or thought and lighten up. It involves not taking things personally or to heart (literally), not taking myself too seriously and realising that every thought and every feeling I experience is meant to simply pass through, not to be held on to. I have no business holding on to any thought or feeling in my life. Experience it fully as it was intended, and then let it go. It is like a wonderful intimate relationship. I must be willing to let it go at any and every moment; only then can I experience deep and passionate intimacy. Grasping or holding on smothers the relationship and any hope of intimacy.

## Speak from the heart – mean what I say and say what I mean

To speak from the heart means to be honest and open while respecting the other person. It is not about being blunt or harsh, aggressive or assertive, loud or overpowering. It is not about being right. It requires a letting go of wanting to influence the listener, to drop my attachment to having things go a particular way (my way). Thus, I am far more likely to experience the other person doing the same. When I am in my heart, then those I meet are more likely to be in theirs. To be in my heart takes courage and a willingness to feel vulnerable. The irony of this is that once I make this decision and do it, I feel far more powerful than when I choose to stay in my head trying to be right or impressive. When I speak from the heart all fear disappears, and I feel a deep connection within me and strength of conviction that can never be mustered from the head. I feel both vulnerable and powerful, being right or wrong becomes irrelevant, words flow and connecting to others is far easier. I am open and fully alive.

## Listen to and follow my heart

It takes a lot of energy to keep the heart closed. Its natural state is to be open. However, by focusing on fears and society's negative messages about the dangers out there I feel it is safer to be guarded and suspicious, cautious and cynical. Heart-centred living is all about joy, love and passion. It is about full expression of myself in ways that encourage others to do and be the same. If I can cultivate my natural ability to listen to and act from my heart, life will be much easier and more pleasurable. The most difficult part of this is making the decision to actually do it. Listening to my heart is the easy bit, trusting it and acting on it is the challenge. Doing what I love in life, following my passions, is being in my heart. I aim for a career that inspires and excites me, because there I will shine, excel and realise my potential. I can start somewhere in some way to bring into my life more of what I love to do. Once I start in whatever small way possible, I create a space for attracting more of what I enjoy in my life. Over time I am doing far more of what makes me feel alive and on purpose. When I listen to my heart I get out of my own way and immediately become my greatest ally and resource.

## Recognise and follow my resistance

Resistance is really a signal to keep going. It's my head telling me to be afraid, very afraid. Yet, if I persist and break through the resistance then great success and achievements are inevitable. If I take my resistance at face value then I will pull back, freeze and procrastinate. This is how missed opportunities happen, how regrets build up and bitterness sets in. Fearing the worst is a bad habit and is always a choice. To live in fear is repressive. It is not about being fearless or a superhero. It is about dropping off the cloak of fear through which I filter life, and donning a cloak of possibilities. Focusing on fears causes me to be blind to these opportunities and so is counterproductive. When I am present and grounded I can engage with life in a way that overcomes the fears inside and achieve great things. In doing this I easily see how groundless my fears are and always have been. The only sure way of overcoming my fears and seeing them for the lies that they are is to take action. Do the opposite to what they are telling me. Call their bluff! Taking calculated risks allows me to feel alive and connected to life. The head is an amazing resource and, used wisely, helps me to achieve my dreams. Unchecked, it can be destructive and repressive. Living in my whole body keeps me in the moment and aware. In this way I can more easily recognise my resistance for what it really is and respond appropriately.

## STOP AND REFLECT

✍ Where and when do you find it easy to go with life's flow?

✍ What distracts you from going with life's flow?

✍ What would be different in your life and in you if you lived this lesson every day?

✍ What aspects of this lesson are the most challenging for you? What makes them so?

✍ List at least six things you can do or include in your daily life to integrate and deepen this lesson.

## Lesson five: engage with life

*'The only way to truly find yourself is to surrender yourself to life, unconditionally'*

This lesson highlights the importance of engaging with life. I can only do this with an open heart, by being willing to give and receive, to contribute and share. In other words, truly living life from the inside out.

## Connect with others

When I put others needs first and decide to find ways to help them using my knowledge and talents, then I am moving towards interdependence. The benefits are many. The more I give, the more I get back in so many ways. Trusting my heart or intuition and acting in ways that affirm others is the surest way to build myself up and realise my potential. Connecting with others is a choice I have in each moment. Instead of focusing on differences between myself and others, I can focus on the similarities, the things we have in common that can bring us closer.

We all have so much in common that the differences between us are actually miniscule. On the surface (of life) it would appear that there are glaring differences between us, but underneath, if we truly look and listen, we soon realise that we are mirrors of each other. Choosing to tell others how much I genuinely love, like or admire them simply because I do is also a powerful way of connecting. When I do this it strengthens both of us and opens our hearts. It is the simple act of giving and sharing.

## Ask people for help, support and feedback

A strong, confident person asks for help when they require it, accepts support when it is offered, and seeks feedback as a means of continual self-development and improvement. This is true interdependence. I ask people whom I trust and respect for their honest feedback and for their advice or support when it feels right. Knowing that nothing is ever personal allows me to interact intimately with others, without fear.

## Love is always from the inside out

I have so much love within me and I allow it to flow from me to those I love. I am comfortable enough in myself to open my heart and feel love. This is love in action, feeling it within myself, being in love, and letting it flow or sharing it with others. This love has no preconditions and demands, no rules or goals. To give it to another freely is reward enough. Love is both a state to be in and a way to behave and communicate with another. It requires little effort and few tools on my part: I merely allow it to happen. I choose to feel this love within me, to focus on my heart and let it do the rest. So simple, it's child's play.

## Exercise and meditation

Some form of exercise at least four times a week is important. The benefits are obvious. Some form of meditation is also valuable for, at the very least, creating a space in the day where I am not interrupted by anyone or anything. Spending time alone is vital. How I meditate is up to me. Both these activities are essential for emotional, physical, mental and spiritual well being

## Lesson six: look in the mirror

'The unexamined life is not worth living'

Socrates

'I must be willing to give up what I am in order to become what I will be'

Albert Einstein

This lesson tells me that life is a constant feedback loop, so be kind, loving, compassionate, forgiving. I am in it all and part of it all. Therefore, in every moment or situation there is opportunity for growth and learning.

## Life is a house of a thousand mirrors

Life is constantly reflecting myself back to me on many levels. My foot reflects my whole body in reflexology, as do the eye and ear in Chinese medicine. The atoms and space of which I am made is mirrored in the planets and space making up the universe. All is mirrored by all. The search for learning and meaning intrigues me. Viktor Frankl found meaning and learning in his experience as a prisoner in Auschwitz concentration camp during World War II, which resulted in his new psychotherapy. There is meaning and learning in everything, nothing is wasted or meaningless. Every moment, encounter and event offers the opportunity to open up and be transformed by the learning and meaning gained through this engagement.

The lessons I need to learn about myself and the life I live are forever hidden in the open, where I would least expect to find them or go looking for them. I struggle to find them and see them because I use the head to search. So I analyse, dissect, scrutinise, detect and theorise. I simply think too much. The one thing I fail to do is to look life straight in the eye – to face it full on. By this I mean to be willing to see the actual reality of the moment rather than what the head or ego would like or prefer it to be. I avoid putting my spin on what the moment is about and instead experience it in a more grounded and simpler way.

Amazing discoveries can be made when I am really willing to learn what is available to me in the moment. Discoveries that appear so obvious when I see them that I wonder how I was blind to them for so long. This is because such insights cannot be seen by the head; they can only be seen with an open heart. This takes courage as it demands a willingness to learn regardless of how difficult the lesson. As life is a mirror or feedback mechanism to me about myself, I look upon each moment as an opportunity to discover more about myself. To discover these lessons which exist all around me, I need to want to learn them, and be present.

The answers to my personal problems are always with me, they are part of the problem, built into it. Seeing the problem is part of this process; seeing the solution requires a different perspective, a new way of viewing myself and the situation. The two are inseparable. So when I define the problem accurately I am more than halfway to finding the solution. The head can do the first step, and then I let the heart guide me in the moment to see the solution. Never dismiss the obvious, as that is where the answers might be. Life has no real hiding places, I just need to want to learn and then ask the right questions.

### The solutions to the problems in my life are simple, but not always easy.

While it is true that life is a mystery, in practical terms it is very straight forward. There are basic laws or principles which when adhered to keep things on track. Problems arise mostly through lack of awareness. All of my problems and challenges in this life have simple and obvious solutions to them. I do not need to be a guru to have the answers to my dilemmas. Life is simple. If I decide to keep it simple (easy, effortless, uncomplicated, undemanding, straightforward, trouble-free), then

I am truly at one with life. However, the head will sabotage this if I am not watchful. It often dismisses simple ideas and solutions as being childish and facile. The head knows how to analyse, assess, solve practical problems, categorise and label things. As a resource, used on its own, it will always be limited in some way. My problems and challenges will become traumas and major dramas if I focus on them using only my head. Bring it back to basics. This means open my heart to the situation and follow my instincts. Remember life holds all its treasures in the open. The secrets to living well and happy are always right in front of me. They are:

- Love those I love
- Tell the truth or else shut up
- Spend only what I have and no more
- Eat when I am hungry and eat what my body wants, not what my head wants
- Drink when I am thirsty
- Do things that inspire me and others

If I resolve to do only these things, my life will become transformed. It all comes down to simple choices. But simple is not the same as easy and that is why I struggle. Of course there are habits, emotional and physical blocks and traumas to face, but all that is part of the journey and they only become mountains if I think too much about them, overanalyse, and turn them into epic journeys of torturous, terrifying trials. Simplicity is key. This involves analysing less, relaxing more and trusting my intuition.

## Choose to grow – there is no growth without loss and no loss without growth

How I perceive myself and this life is entirely up to me. I can choose to focus on the things that I fear, that frustrate me, annoy me, or intimidate me. Or I can focus on the things that calm me, cheer me up, inspire and excite me. Every situation in life offers me the choice to take the personal learning from it or take it personally and dramatise it. The former choice brings awareness and growth, the latter resistance and stagnation. To grow means to let go of the old ways and embrace the new learning. It is trust in action, stepping out of the comfort zone over and over, losing the familiar to grow. I can only grow through letting go, through losing that which was me. Life is about cycles of growth, I choose to go with the flow of life and grow with it as it teaches me.

### STOP AND REFLECT

- Where and when do you find it easy to look in the mirror?

- What distracts you from looking in the mirror?

- What would be different in your life and in you if you lived this lesson every day?

- What aspects of this lesson are the most challenging for you? What makes them so?

- List at least six things you can do or include in your daily life to integrate and deepen this lesson.

## The Process: follow the yellow brick road

*Tin Woodsman*: What have you learned, Dorothy?

*Dorothy*: Well, I – I think that it – it wasn't enough to just want to see Uncle Henry and Auntie Em – and it's that – if I ever go looking for my heart's desire again, I won't look any further than my own backyard. Because if it isn't there, I never really lost it to begin with! Is that right?

(The Wizard of Oz, 1939)

Dorothy, in the movie *The Wizard of Oz*, was told to follow the yellow brick road to reach her goal of getting home. On this journey towards her goal she meets many strange characters and has some unnerving experiences. Everything that happens to her and everyone she meets on this road is telling her something about herself and the journey she is on. The courage, heart and intelligence desired by the characters who join her on this journey are all within them already. Just like Dorothy, who is looking to go home, they all go looking for their deepest desires outside of themselves. They believe that the wizard will fix them, give them all the answers they need in life and make them happy. Dumb or what?!

I was Dorothy. Like her I wanted others to fix me, to tell me how to get home, to get back to me, where I would feel at peace and accepted. I journeyed on the road rigidly focused on the goal of happiness and enlightenment, totally miserable as I travelled. Consequently, I was missing the only thing that mattered: the journey. Always, I looked straight ahead, into the distance, waiting for something to happen, seeking out the wizard to get me home.

Eventually I realised that, like all the characters travelling the yellow brick road, I was ignoring the obvious. What I was looking for was inside me all along. I had never left home. All I was seeking and longing for was within me from the very start. Travelling along the road taught me that. We discover ourselves by stepping onto the path of life and following it. In so many ways life is speaking to us; nothing is irrelevant or so small that we can dismiss it. Everything has meaning. All around us are opportunities to learn and grow.

Other people's lives are rich in lessons for each of us to learn from. Take Maura Murphy who spent most of her life rearing her large family in poverty in the midlands of Ireland. Then, in her seventies, she was diagnosed with cancer. She took this news as a wake-up call and acted on it. She separated from her husband and wrote her memoir. Her book *Don't Wake Me At Doyle's* became a bestseller in the UK and Ireland and Maura recovered fully from her cancer. There are many lessons one can take from this episode of Maura's life. An obvious one is not to wait for life to threaten you with death before you wake up and follow your heart. Make sure you reach the end of your journey with as few regrets as possible.

While we all have fear in us, courage is also residing within us. We cannot have one without the other. Choosing to focus on our courage rather than our fear makes all the difference. A strong heart can overcome anything. Remember you are the only one who can experience your life. So do it with a full and open heart. Life will honour and reward you for this in ways you cannot even imagine or at least that your head can't even imagine! Do not underestimate the power of your own heart.

The yellow brick road, your journey in life, can be a scary and stressful one to travel or it can be an exciting and inspiring road to be on. That choice is always yours to make. Part of this journey we all take is about self-acceptance. We never will be perfect, nor should we try to be. Self-acceptance is an act of compassion towards ourselves and when we can do this others around us will automatically benefit. It is always our choice; to reject who we are in this moment, fight with ourselves and travel the world trying to fix or find ourselves or open up and accept who we are in this moment and in doing so begin to improve those aspects of our lives and ourselves that we know in our hearts need to change.

True self-help therefore is the act of unconditional acceptance of the self, an opening up to all that life presents to and through us. From this place anything is possible.

# Appendix

This section contains three exercises designed to assist you in identifying the specific aspects of the life lessons that you need to improve the practice of and how to practically achieve this.

## Exercise 3a

The Life Lessons Wheel – This provides a broad overview of your current position in relation to how effective the life lessons are being applied in your life. It is a snapshot of the big picture. To what extent if any, are the life lessons being consciously applied by you? From this useful starting point you can quickly gauge your weak spots that require immediate attention.

It can be completed several times over a specific period to monitor progress as you work on practicing the lessons, making them part of your regular life experience.

## Exercise 3b

Life Lessons Self Assessment – This instrument takes each section of the Life Lessons Wheel and examines them in greater detail, asking you to rate your response to a series of statements designed to identify key issues that are contributing to low scores on the Life Lessons Wheel.

The section totals should reflect to some degree the initial high/low self-scores you gave on the Life Lessons Wheel. However, these exercises are subjective in nature and will only have any real meaning for you. There are no right or wrong answers. You decide what is appropriate for you.

Next choose specific items which received a low rating to focus on, with the aim of raising their rating.

## Exercise 3c

Life Lessons Applied – Plan of Action – This builds on the previous two exercises, providing you with a template to create goals and action plans for effective and comprehensive implementation of the life lessons in your daily life.

## *Exercise 3a*

## Life Lessons Wheel

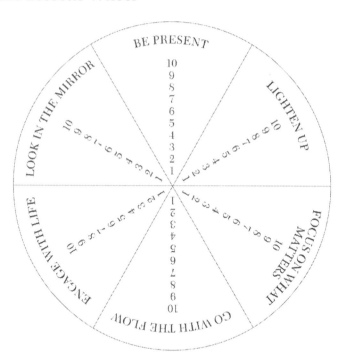

Complete the chart by marking where your current level of satisfaction is for each of the life lessons in terms of how well you apply them in your daily life.

(1 = totally dissatisfied. 10 = completely satisfied)

Once you have completed the chart, connect the points. Fill in the dates below. Monitor your progress by updating the chart at regular intervals.

| | |
|---|---|
| Today's date:_____ | Date(6 months):_____ |
| Date(3 months):_____ | Date(12 months):_____ |

## Exercise 3b

## How Open Am I?

## Life Lessons Self-assessment

- ↳ The following table consists of the six life lessons. Each lesson contains four strategies for applying it. Rate yourself from 1 to 5 on how often you use each of the strategies – (1 = never; 2 = rarely; 3 = sometimes 4 = often; 5 = always)

- ↳ Total the four scores for each lesson. Then halve that total for a final total score for each life lesson. You will finish with six total scores which can be compared with the scores you gave yourself on the Life Lessons wheel.

| Lesson | Strategies | Self-rating Scale | | | | |
|---|---|---|---|---|---|---|
| 1<br>Be Present | I go through my day slowly | 1 | 2 | 3 | 4 | 5 |
| | I feel and express my emotions | 1 | 2 | 3 | 4 | 5 |
| | I breathe deeply | 1 | 2 | 3 | 4 | 5 |
| | I easily accept what is now | 1 | 2 | 3 | 4 | 5 |
| | Total Score /2 | | | | | |
| 2<br>Lighten Up | I laugh daily | 1 | 2 | 3 | 4 | 5 |
| | I choose to have fun and feel joy often | 1 | 2 | 3 | 4 | 5 |
| | I like being curious | 1 | 2 | 3 | 4 | 5 |
| | I practise being defenceless | 1 | 2 | 3 | 4 | 5 |
| | Total Score /2 | | | | | |

## Open

| 3<br>Focus on what matters | I accept and appreciate my own uniqueness | 1 | 2 | 3 | 4 | 5 |
|---|---|---|---|---|---|---|
| | I easily recognise my own achievements | 1 | 2 | 3 | 4 | 5 |
| | I choose my attitude to people and events around me | 1 | 2 | 3 | 4 | 5 |
| | I listen to and trust my intuition | 1 | 2 | 3 | 4 | 5 |
| *Total Score /2* | | | | | | |
| 4<br>Go with life's flow | I can easily let go in each moment | 1 | 2 | 3 | 4 | 5 |
| | I speak from my heart | 1 | 2 | 3 | 4 | 5 |
| | I listen to and follow my heart | 1 | 2 | 3 | 4 | 5 |
| | I recognise and follow my resistance | 1 | 2 | 3 | 4 | 5 |
| *Total Score /2* | | | | | | |
| 5<br>Engage with life | I easily connect with others | 1 | 2 | 3 | 4 | 5 |
| | I accept and give help and feedback | 1 | 2 | 3 | 4 | 5 |
| | I love from the inside out | 1 | 2 | 3 | 4 | 5 |
| | I exercise and meditate | 1 | 2 | 3 | 4 | 5 |
| *Total Score /2* | | | | | | |
| 6<br>Look in the mirror | I focus on the message, not the messenger (I know it is never personal) | 1 | 2 | 3 | 4 | 5 |
| | I find the solutions to my problems are always simple and obvious (solutions are beyond the problem) | 1 | 2 | 3 | 4 | 5 |
| | I take time to reflect | 1 | 2 | 3 | 4 | 5 |
| | I choose growth – I focus on the process, rather than the outcome | 1 | 2 | 3 | 4 | 5 |
| *Total Score /2* | | | | | | |

| Sections | 1 | 2 | 3 | 4 | 5 | 6 |
|---|---|---|---|---|---|---|
| Section totals | | | | | | |

The section totals are simple gross indicators of your level of satisfaction regarding the practce of that lesson in your life currently. Certain strategies may get a score of 3 or lower. These may warrant further consideration if you wish to strengthen the presence of that lesson in your life.

Compare these results with the original Life Lessons Wheel scores.

## Exercise 3c

## Opening Up

## Life Lessons Applied – Plan of Action

The following table consists of the six life lessons. Each lesson contains the same four strategies for applying it. For each strategy identify two activities that you can adopt to implement that strategy effectively, which in turn ensures the successful realisation of that life lesson in your life

## OPEN

| Lesson | Strategies | Exercise/Activity |
|---|---|---|
| 1 Be Present | I go through my day slowly | 1_____ 2_____ |
| | I feel and express my emotions | 1_____ 2_____ |
| | I breathe deeply | 1_____ 2_____ |
| | I easily accept what is now | 1_____ 2_____ |
| 2 Lighten Up | I laugh daily | 1_____ 2_____ |
| | I choose to have fun and joy often | 1_____ 2_____ |
| | I like being curious | 1_____ 2_____ |
| | I practise being defenceless | 1_____ 2_____ |
| 3 Focus on what matters | I accept and appreciate my own uniqueness | 1_____ 2_____ |
| | I easily recognise my own achievements | 1_____ 2_____ |
| | I choose my Attitude to people and events around me | 1_____ 2_____ |
| | I listen to and trust my intuition | 1_____ 2_____ |
| 4 Go with life's flow | I can easily let go in each moment | 1_____ 2_____ |
| | I speak from my heart | 1_____ 2_____ |
| | I listen to and follow my heartt | 1_____ 2_____ |
| | I recognise and follow my resistance | 1_____ 2_____ |

| | | |
|---|---|---|
| 5<br>Engage<br>with life | I easily connect with others | 1_____<br>2_____ |
| | I accept and give help and feedback | 1_____<br>2_____ |
| | I Love from the inside out | 1_____<br>2_____ |
| | I exercise and meditate | 1_____<br>2_____ |
| 6<br>Look<br>in The<br>Mirror | I focus on the message, not the messenger<br>(I know it is never personal!) | 1_____<br>2_____ |
| | I find the solutions to my problems are always simple and obvious<br>(Solutions are beyond the problem) | 1_____<br>2_____ |
| | I take time to reflect | 1_____<br>2_____ |
| | I choose growth – I focus on the process, rather than the outcome | 1_____<br>2_____ |